THE TRIANGLE

THE TRIANGLE

A Year on the Ground with New York's Bloods and Crips

KEVIN DEUTSCH

Lyons Press
Guilford, Connecticut
Helena, Montana
An imprint of Rowman & Littlefield

Lyons Press is an imprint of Rowman & Littlefield

Distributed by NATIONAL BOOK NETWORK

Copyright © 2014 by Kevin Deutsch
Map by Amy McDevitt

British Library Cataloguing-in-Publication Information available

Library of Congress Cataloging-in-Publication Data

Deutsch, Kevin.
  The triangle : a year on the ground with New York's Bloods and Crips / Kevin Deutsch.
    pages cm
  ISBN 978-1-4930-0760-8 (pbk.)
  1. Gangs--New York (State)--New York. 2. African American criminals--New York (State)--New York. 3. Bloods (Gang) 4. Crips (Gang) I. Title.
  HV6439.U7N437 2014
  364.106'609747245--dc23
                                    2014030906

∞™ The paper used in this publication meets the minimum requirements of American National Standard for Information Sciences—Permanence of Paper for Printed Library Materials, ANSI/NISO Z39.48-1992.

For my mother and father

The following is a work of nonfiction. All the events chronicled in these pages were either witnessed firsthand by the author or alleged during interviews with his subjects. In order to protect the identities of gang members, crime victims, law enforcement officials, and other interviewees, most of their names have been changed. For that same reason, some locations and other identifying details have been obscured.

CONTENTS

AUTHOR'S NOTE

This is the story of a gang war fought in 2012 between the Bloods and Crips in Hempstead, Long Island, New York. It is about the men, women, and children caught up in that conflict, and the struggles they faced while living and fighting in a suburban war zone.

All the events chronicled in these pages were either witnessed by me or alleged during interviews with my subjects. In order to protect the identities of gang members, crime victims, law enforcement officials, and other interviewees, most of their names have been changed. For that same reason, some locations and other identifying details have been obscured.

I risked my life on multiple occasions to gather the information in this book, but those I wrote about risked their lives every day—some in an effort to kill their enemies, some in an effort to stop the killing, and others, simply to get to work, raise their children, and make it through the day. In every war, there are heroes. Hempstead's good citizens—the ones who refuse to give up on their community despite the daily horrors witnessed there—are the heroes of this one.

Kevin Deutsch
Hempstead, Long Island
June 2014

List of Key Players

BLOODS

Michael "Ice" Williams—Set Leader

Joe "Steed" Wallace—Lieutenant

Arthur "Doc" Reed—Second Lieutenant

Jerome "Big Mac" McDaniel—Enforcer

Lamar Crawford—Rackets Supervisor

Devon "D-Bo" LaFleur—Corner Supervisor

James "J-Roc" Pendleton—Corner Boy

Derek "Big Boy" Owens—Corner Boy

"Super Curt" Ellis—Corner Boy

CRIPS

Tyrek Singleton—Set Leader

Anthony "Big Tony" Sherman—Lieutenant

Gary "Flex" Butler—Second Lieutenant

Joey "Rock" James—Enforcer

"Bolo Jay" Woodson—Corner Boy/Enforcer

Tevin "Dice" Beckles—Corner Supervisor

Savant Sharpe—Corner Boy

Skinny Pete—Corner Boy

GLOSSARY OF TERMS

Big Homie—A high-ranking Crips member

Burner—A disposable cell phone used by gang members to discuss business

Cookhouse—Location where powder cocaine is cooked into crack

Corner Boy—A low-ranking gang member who sells drugs. Touts, runners, and lookouts are all corner boys.

Death Day—A party held in honor of a deceased gang member

Hitter—A trained killer who carries out assassinations and enforcement for his gang

Iron—A handgun

Lookout—A gang member who stands guard on drug corners, looking for police and enemy crews

Mission—A task assigned to a gang member, often requiring violence

Pipehead—A crack addict

Rock—Crack cocaine

Runner—A gang member who retrieves drugs from a crew's hidden stash whenever an order is made. Some runners also transport drugs between cookhouses and stash houses.

Slob—Derogatory term for a Blood, often used by Crips in conversation

Soldier—A participant in the gang war

Stash House/Spot—Location where cocaine or marijuana is stored by gang members

Top Homie—A Crips set leader

Tout—A gang member who promotes his crew's daily drug selections and steers customers toward dealers

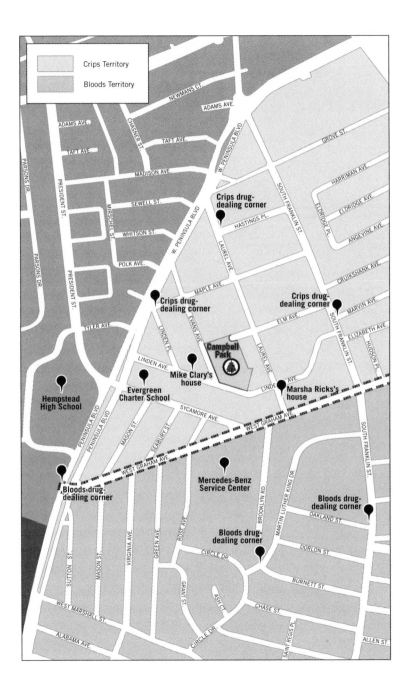

CHAPTER ONE

Opening Salvo

January 2012
Hempstead, Long Island
New York

Somebody going to come out on top. Ain't no ties in this here game.
—Flex

As he watches a car full of rival drug dealers drive down Linden Avenue, Gary "Flex" Butler adjusts the Glock nine-millimeter in his waistband, exhales a long stream of marijuana smoke, and shakes his head in disgust.

"Those boys don't learn," Butler, eighteen, says of the baby-faced men in the beige, late-model Lincoln Town Car, which turns slowly down Linden Place before disappearing into the night. "They hit us, we hit them. They don't stop coming."

The "boys" he speaks of are rival drug dealers—Bloods gang members who had ventured off their turf on nearby Martin Luther King Jr. Drive to send a message to Butler and his friends in the local Crips crew. They want it known that an ongoing war between their groups would continue, Butler says, despite the recent rumors that a truce had been called.

"Ain't no peace," he says. "Nothing of the sort."

Four young men in Butler's crew pile into a cranberry-colored Cadillac and drive east, past their rival set's hangout half a mile way. He watches them go, declaring that another shooting could happen anytime.

"That's how it is," says Butler. "Almost every night now."

An hour later, on MLK Drive, a Bloods dealing crew is huddled in a doorway of the project building that serves as their unofficial headquarters. There are seven in the crew and another six patrolling their territory in a black SUV. The gangsters in the doorway pass blunts of weed laced with coke to one another, nodding their heads to the Lil Wayne song— "Enemy Turf"—blasting from the radio at their feet.

One of the Bloods, Arthur "Doc" Reed, twenty-five, runs his hand along the bandage wrapped around his stomach. He'd been shot in his right abdomen a week earlier; the nine-millimeter bullet narrowly missed an artery. Released from the hospital just a few hours ago, Doc's still wearing the blue intensive-care bracelet on his thin, tattooed wrist.

"Niggas need to pay, you feel me?" Doc says.

He's addressing one of the crew's top-ranking members, a twenty-six-year-old Los Angeles native named Joe "Steed" Wallace. Steed, a longtime West Coast Blood, is credited with helping turn the Hempstead set into a regional force. He nods his head and spits into the street, fingering the scar on his chin the way he does sometimes when he's angry. He'd been touching it as a reminder to himself ever since a car full of Crips drove by an hour earlier, slowing to a crawl as they passed while eyeballing Steed and his crew.

"I feel you, but we going to do this shit on our terms," Steed tells Doc and the others. "Aight?"

"Hell yeah," says Doc. "So, like, how?"

"Wait for my word," Steed says, going at the scar again. So they wait.

Police, residents, and the gang members themselves refer to the neighborhood both crews call home as a "war zone." They're not exaggerating. Mike Clary, a Hempstead native and marine who came home in 2010 after serving three tours in the Iraq War, said he "felt right at home when I came back, because there were just as many bullets and screams here as there were some days over there.

"I was in Fallujah when it was a shit show, at its absolute worse. And this reminds me of those bad months over there. The kids screaming. The gunshots at all hours. The fear you feel just walking down to the corner store. Those are the same experiences you have in Iraq."

Except this war on Clary's street is all about drug territory, and a gang rivalry with forty-five years of bitter history.

Hempstead Crips control the market for marijuana and cocaine in the area surrounding Linden Avenue and Linden Place—a blighted, impoverished area known as the Linden Triangle, or simply the Triangle—on the north side of West Graham Avenue. South of Graham, on MLK Drive, the local Bloods set controls a smaller drug market in and around the housing projects lining the street. Both crews want to take over each other's drug markets. As for strategies, they seem to have settled on a war of attrition, aiming to kill or maim as many of their enemies as possible until one side can no longer fight.

For a village of roughly 55,000 people, even one whose residents are long accustomed to living among violence, the amount of bloodshed here is remarkable. Between 2007 and 2011, 186 people were shot in the village—about half of them in connection with feuds involving the Bloods and Crips.

And the violence only grows worse in the new year. During the first weeks of the 2012 gang war, a sixteen-year-old boy partially loses his sight when an errant nine-millimeter bullet grazes his right eye. Another child loses an ear. A third has two fingers blown off when a stray round blows through his bedroom window and strikes him as he reads *The Cat in the Hat* in bed.

And that's just in January.

The gangs have two things going for them that make both unwilling to accept defeat. First, each is able to buy top-quality cocaine directly from major traffickers at wholesale prices, as little as $17,000 per kilo compared with the average going price of about $23,000. The second is that they're far better armed and willing to use violence than the smaller neighborhood cliques scattered throughout Nassau County. Authorities say the Crips and Bloods can compete successfully on price and purity on their corners throughout Long Island, making huge profits even while splitting their primary market in Hempstead. They're also able to keep out other competitors through use of brute force.

Then there's the matter of battlefield geography. The Triangle, as its name suggests, contains three angles, meaning whichever gang controls it has unobstructed views of every vehicle and person approaching or leaving a corner. Such terrain is ideal for drug dealers, since it steals the element of surprise from police as well as enemy gangs. As a result, the Bloods want to conquer it as badly as the Crips want to hold it.

"Somebody going to come out on top," Flex Butler says of the conflict. "Ain't no ties in this here game."

A tie is exactly what Reverend Kirk Lyons is praying for, a truce that will bring peace to his old neighborhood. The fifty-one-year-old Hempstead native, who everyone simply calls The Reverend, had recently finished a successful outreach campaign with gang members in Newark, New Jersey, when some of his old friends called with disturbing news: A war between the Bloods and Crips was laying waste to his hometown, and his help was urgently needed.

Lyons, who has dedicated his life to stopping young black men from needlessly killing each other, agreed to intervene. He decided to employ a novel strategy: midnight prayer marches in which a small group of male, middle-aged Hempstead residents-turned-activists walk through the village's war-torn drug markets, looking for gang members and addicts with whom to pray.

Many of the marchers Lyons rounds up for his mission are former junkies or gang members themselves, having once sowed mayhem on the same streets they now find themselves trying to clean up. For some, the marches serve as a form of penance, a way of showing contrition for the pain they caused their families, friends, and neighbors in their youth. Others sign up to march out of anger or grief, fed up with the shootings and retaliatory strikes; the seemingly endless funeral processions; and the twin plagues of easy-to-buy guns and plentiful crack engulfing their hometown.

Despite their best intentions, things don't begin well for the men. On the first night they march, a group of Crips goes on war footing when they see them approaching the corner of Linden Avenue and Linden Place—the heart of the Triangle, and a busy spot where the gang sells coke and

The sinister plots hatched by one gang against the other don't stop. But neither do Reverend Kirk Lyons (at center) and his prayer marchers. They return to the Triangle every Friday just before midnight to pray with gang members, always with the goal of preventing retaliatory attacks.
STEVE PFOST

weed. The Crips form a human wall, a "battle formation," as Lyons calls it, and aggressively march toward the older men. Lyons doesn't know why the dealers have been provoked so quickly, until he looks down and sees his shirt is red, as are those of several other marchers.

"Stop," he tells his men. "They think we're Bloods."

But it's too late. The gangsters meet them in the middle of the street, chests stuck out, eyes wide with anger. It doesn't take much more than wearing the wrong color to get shot in the Triangle, the marchers know.

Lyons quickly explains they're here to pray, not fight.

"It was a mistake," he tells the Crips.

The young men look skeptical. A few of their hands slide down to their waistbands, lifting shirts to reveal flashes of chrome. Lyons, who's seen plenty of guns in his day, keeps his cool. He introduces his marchers one by one, and each man in turn reaches out and shakes hands with each of the gang members. The marchers are all either balding or have beer bellies. Most wear what one marcher calls "dad jeans," in stark contrast to the ultra-baggy, low-riding pants worn by the Crips. The gang members seem to notice the difference. Realizing the men pose no threat, they relax.

"No red next time," one of the Crips says. "This the only pass you going to get."

"No red," Lyons says.

The gangsters return to their corner to sell drugs while the marchers continue on. Despite the shaky start, they return every Friday shortly before midnight, meeting outside the All Saints Temple Church of God in Christ on Laurel Avenue and walking through both crews' territories during peak business hours. Some weeks, they march down blocks where a gun battle would almost certainly break out if not for their presence.

"In that way alone, we feel we're making a difference," Lyons says. "We understand the risks we're taking."

But the risks are about to become much greater.

CHAPTER TWO

The Shop

This here beef we having is like some corporate fight you'd read about in the Wall Street Journal, *only this about our kind of business: rock cocaine.*

—Ice

Anthony "Big Tony" Sherman is twenty-two, with a baby on the way. He'd served two years in an upstate prison for selling cocaine before coming home eight months ago. His first night back in Hempstead, he got his girlfriend pregnant.

"Doctor said it's a boy," Tony says. "Going to be my prince. He'll be nothing but blessed."

Tony is standing on the stoop of a run-down apartment building on Linden Place, which serves as the Crips' clubhouse while doubling as the primary location from which they sell and stash crack, powder cocaine, and marijuana. He supervises the Shop—as the Crips' main drug market is known—making sure the gang's dealing crews throughout the area have enough coke and weed to meet the day's demands. Shortly after sunrise, customers begin to arrive, anxious to see what kind of product the crew is slinging. All around them, students are walking to one of two schools near the Triangle: Hempstead High School and Evergreen Charter School. Most do their best to ignore the gangsters' pitches. Others stop to cop, wanting to get lit before homeroom.

"Got that Luda!" one Crip shouts to a pair of junkies walking down the block.

"Come get that Notorious!" cries another gangster at an approaching car.

"Yeah, business going to be good today," Tony says. "Weekend coming, so we opening a little early. Fiends be getting prepared. And I gots to get this money for the baby. Crib, diapers, clothes, all that stuff. My child going to be mad spoiled."

The customers walk or drive up expectantly, ready to sample the Crips' offerings. Tony's sure the Luda crack vials and baggies will be big sellers, likely to surpass the Notorious viles and baggies as the crew's most popular products. The night before, he'd passed out free samples to a couple of local junkies who serve as the crew's product testers. They'd assured him the rocks had them good and lit—some of the best crack they'd ever procured in the neighborhood. They must have been telling the truth, because one of them, Charlie Bones, is among the first to walk up to the Crips shop this morning when it opens for business.

"Let me get that Luda, twenty hard," Charlie says, ordering a $20 crack rock. "That shit's the bomb."

He hands over a wrinkled, yellow-tinged $20 bill to Tevin "Dice" Beckles, who's handling tout duties for the Crips this morning. Touts promote the day's drug selections, barking out product names and extolling their virtues to any potential customers within earshot. They also accept payment from each fiend and make sure all the cash is there.

"Damn nigga, you pee on this bill?" Dice says, holding up the $20 bill between two fingers like a dirty sock. "Shit is nasty."

"Nah yo, that was my change at the store," Charlie says, nodding toward the bodega up the street. "Ain't nobody peed on it. Just old is all."

Dice holds the bill up for closer inspection, gives it a sniff, and, seemingly satisfied it has not been pissed on, stuffs it in his pocket.

"Aight, but don't be bringing them nasty bills over here no more," Dice says.

Charlie, his hands beginning to tremble for want of a fix, grunts his affirmation; Dice directs him toward the side of an apartment building.

Charlie waits there as Dice flashes a hand sign to Skinny Pete, a rail-thin seventeen-year-old handling runner duties today. Runners retrieve drugs from a drug crew's hidden stash whenever an order is made and are usually the skinniest kids in their set because of all the exercise. Pete, seeing Dice's hand sign, runs around the back of the building and returns with a baggie full of gumball-size crack rocks.

"This some high-quality raw right here," Pete says, marveling at the product's apparent quality.

Savant Sharpe, an eighteen-year-old aspiring rapper working as the crew's lookout today, watches the street for any approaching cops or Bloods. Declaring the coast clear, he nods to Pete, who hands the baggie to Charlie. The fiend eyes it gratefully before sliding it into his sock and strolling off, whistling the opening notes to Marvin Gaye's "Sexual Healing."

This routine—with touts, runners, and lookouts all doing their part—will play itself out hundreds of times today on Long Island drug corners operated by Crips and Bloods. Thousands more crack and weed transactions will be made by the gangs' sets across the country—part of a lucrative, wartime economic system still going strong nearly four decades after crack, a cheap, addictive form of cocaine, appeared in the United States.

"Another satisfied customer," Tony says, watching Charlie walk off with his morning fix.

"We going to make bank of this batch," says his deputy, Flex Butler.

Tony is the crew's top street-level dealer and day-to-day manager. Flex, a jack-of-all-trades for the Crips, who handles everything from enforcement to package price negotiations, is ranked just below him in the gang's hierarchy. Flex calls Tony on the phone or consults with him face-to-face in the gang's clubhouse whenever a ruling on some pressing matter is needed. Tony, meanwhile, answers to the leader of the Hempstead Crips, a man named Tyrek Singleton. Depending on whom you ask, Tyrek is either the most ruthless, sadistic gangster in the New York metropolitan area or a gentleman hustler who runs his drug business more like Bill Gates than Scarface. "The man is a scary mothafucka," Tony says. "And smart as hell, too." Seeking insulation from his crew's criminal activities, Tyrek typically stays off the streets. Tony is in constant contact with him, keeping him abreast of supply issues, daily profit margins, information about police presence in the area, and any fresh intelligence on the Bloods.

"If I hear they [the Bloods] about to make a move, any move, I tell Tyrek," Tony says.

Tony sees himself as a businessman, partnered with Tyrek and other leaders in the Crips organization—Big Homies, as they're known in Crips parlance—in a joint effort to recruit talent, maximize profits, and expand their customer base.

"We're looking to market, sell, and profit off drugs the way any business would handle their product," Tony says. "Only our product is illegal, so more precautions need to be taken. It's all systematic and planned, all the positions and responsibilities and assignments. All of that's part of our business strategy. It's usually real smooth and quiet, because that's the best environment for us to make bank. But now, we at war, man. Ain't nothing quiet these days."

The father-to-be often contemplates his own death, knowing it could come at any time now that full-scale armed conflict has broken out in the neighborhood. But he doesn't worry much about the prospect of his son growing up without him.

"If I fall, my niggas going to take care of him like he's their own. That's how we do. We ain't just an army. We ain't just a business. We a family."

Inside the "clubhouse" apartment where Tyrek, Tony, and the rest of the Crips spend much of their downtime, there are few hints that the space is a hub for crack dealing. The place is sparsely decorated, with a Notorious B.I.G. poster hanging in the living room beside a dartboard and Nerf basketball hoop. Wooden chairs and metal tables are scattered across the room for card playing and dominoes. Massive speakers and a sixty-inch plasma flat-screen television sit atop an entertainment center in the corner farthest from the door. The gangsters play a continuous stream of hip-hop on the speakers via Bluetooth setups on their smartphones, taking turns providing playlists. Rick Ross, Nas, Odd Future, Jay Z, 2Pac, Biggie, and Wu-Tang Clan are on heavy rotation. The TV is tuned to local news all day, so that the Crips can stay abreast of Hempstead's latest shootings.

"Anybody gets shot around here, they put it on TV," Flex says. "Nine times out of ten, we know the person. So we try and pay attention to it."

"Sometimes, the stories be all about us," Tony says.

There have been news reports of shootings and stabbings almost daily since the two sets began their war earlier this month. The police department's gunfire recognition system, called ShotSpotter, registered so many gunshots in the area at one point that cops thought it might be malfunctioning. Today's been quiet so far, but Tony believes that won't be the case much longer.

"Sooner or later, they going to come for Dice," Tony says.

Dice Beckles, the Crips tout, is widely thought to have shot Doc Reed, the high-ranking Bloods dealer, two weeks earlier. Tony believes a retaliatory shooting will be carried out by the Bloods at some point in the coming days, so he's summoned several Big Homies to the clubhouse in order to talk strategy and weigh their options.

"Problem is, we don't know when those niggas coming," Tony tells them. "That means y'all got to be ready at all times. Do not leave home without a piece. And roll out in numbers, aight?"

The others nod. Some look no older than fifteen. Others are seventeen or eighteen and have either dropped out of high school or will before the school year is out. All wear sagging jeans with shirts from top-end designers and $200 high-tops. And each carries a blue handkerchief, a long-standing Crips tradition among the gang's thousands of sets across the country.

"Aight," says Dice, who's wearing a bulletproof vest beneath his blue Yankees jersey in anticipation of a Bloods' assassination attempt on his life. "But five-o be out there in force right now. How we handling that?"

"Just keep doing what you doing and don't worry about the police," Tony says. "They just making a show, peacocking and shit, but there ain't nothing to worry about as long as you stay smart. They rolling through the hood more than usual because they expect shit to pop off at some point.

But they a small-ass force, yo. Hempstead PD ain't got the manpower to be up in our shit twenty-four/seven. And they ain't got no undercovers they can get past us."

By the police department's own admission, Tony's probably right. The force is undermanned and underfunded, the village still reeling from the Great Recession. It's also true that the police have failed to infiltrate either the Hempstead Bloods or Crips with undercovers in the past. So as long as the gang's members keep their mouths shut, Tony tells them, no major cases can be made.

"If you get picked up by five-o, just shut the fuck up, sit there, and wait for us to get you out," Tony says. "Tyrek will take care of bail, lawyers, everything. You just carry that shit like a soldier."

His address to the troops complete, Tony nods at Flex, who pulls out a garbage bag full of still-packaged burners—the hard-to-trace phones gang members often use to talk business—and dumps them onto a table.

"Everybody take one," Flex says. "And use them shits wisely."

⚊⚋⚊

While the Crips wait on a retaliatory strike against Dice, the Bloods brain trust plots one. The leader of the local Bloods set, Michael "Ice" Williams, twenty-four, has summoned Steed Wallace, Doc Reed, Lamar Crawford, and several other members to Seduccion, a Hempstead strip club used by the gang as an occasional meeting spot.

Sipping on Hennessy at a table beside the stage, Ice tells his men they'll exact revenge for Doc's shooting by going after Dice, but not for another four nights.

"Today's Friday, and the cops probably going to be beefing up patrols tonight and all weekend," Ice says. "Come Monday, most likely they'll scale shit back. Tuesday, they'll be even less of them. That's the night we ride out."

Doc lobbies for an assignment as triggerman for the mission, since he's familiar with Dice's daily routine and wants to avenge his own shooting. In the Triangle, if an enemy gang member tries to kill you, the only acceptable response is to return the favor.

The now-defunct Seduccion gentleman's club was used by the Bloods as a meeting spot for strategy sessions during the gang war.
KEVIN DEUTSCH

"Dice usually be smoking weed on the stoop of his cousin's house after school," Doc says. "We could just drive past and take that nigga out real easy."

Steed says he's obtained a semiautomatic TEC-9 for the drive-by from a Bloods associate—someone who works for the gang but is not yet an official member—per Ice's orders. As far as Steed knows, the gun is unregistered and untraceable. The TEC-9 has recently become the Bloods' go-to weapon for drive-by shootings, mostly because they're cheap and plentiful on the black market. They also hold a thirty-two-bullet cartridge, increasing the chances that at least one round will strike an intended target, however inept the triggerman.

"You ever handled a semiauto?" Steed asks Doc. "Ain't no fucking toy."

"Ain't no piece I can't handle," Doc says.

Steed looks to Ice, who nods in approval of the plan, making it official. The Bloods leader then turns to his protégé, Lamar Crawford, whose main job these days is running the Bloods' prostitution racket.

Ice tells Lamar that he wants him to "handle the management end" of the drive-by. "You and Doc together on this. You need another soldier or some other issue come up, let Steed know," Ice says.

A broad-shouldered nineteen-year-old who recently graduated from Hempstead High School, Lamar is considered one of the set's smartest, most capable members. He'd handled corner dealing, lookout, and runner duties before taking over the crew's burgeoning prostitution business and is now being groomed to take on more responsibility. Ice has made Lamar's professional development a personal project of sorts, gradually moving him up in the gang's hierarchy in accordance with his annual progress in school. As a freshman, he'd been a lowly messenger. Now, a few weeks after earning a diploma, he's been chosen to take part in an important assassination mission, which will have repercussions for months after the shots ring out.

"You ready to step up?" Ice says.

"Mos def," says Lamar.

Once their meeting ends, the Bloods watch as several dancers gyrate onstage, inviting customers to slide bills into their G-strings. The young women focus nearly all their attention on Ice, like he's some kind of celebrity. Around here, according to Hempstead residents and fellow gang members, he is. No gangland figure in the neighborhood, with the possible exception of Tyrek Singleton, commands more admiration or fear. Ice is thought to be one of the wealthiest, most powerful men in the community. Unlike most of the local Bloods and Crips, Ice attended college and earned a bachelor's degree in accounting. His own education was one of the reasons he'd made a point of ushering Lamar up through the ranks as he advanced in school.

"Intelligence is important, education is important, putting your mind to good use is important," Ice says. "That's why I'm bringing Lamar along . . . he's got book smarts to go with street smarts."

Ice speaks often of authors he's read, from Frederick Douglass and Richard Wright to Sun Tzu and Machiavelli. He'd had plenty of time to absorb the classics while serving five years in prison for selling crack. Despite having a degree, Ice's rap sheet is as long as those of the high-school dropouts who populate most of Hempstead's drug corners. Like many Bloods and Crips, he'd also survived a gunshot wound—a bullet to his left ankle that left him with a permanent limp.

"I ain't no saint and I ain't no genius, but I'll sometimes give books to the younger niggas who show potential, talk to them about philosophy, history, everything," Ice says. "Most of them won't finish high school, because they like making money out here too much. I respect that, too. That's capitalism. But I try to educate them when I can."

Ice says his pursuit of an education in accounting stemmed from his long-running interest in business and a natural acumen for deal making. After graduation, he'd languished in a low-level job with a financial firm in New Jersey. He moved on to a similar job at a more prestigious company in Manhattan, but his bosses rarely let him do any real accounting work, instead turning him into a glorified gopher who fetched their coffee in between menial assignments.

"I believe my skin color held me back when I tried to pursue a career in accounting and finance," Ice says. "I was not allowed to work at the level I was capable of; because I'm black, I was seen as less capable."

Eventually, Ice was laid off. Broke and jobless, he returned to the Park Lake apartments on MLK where he'd grown up, and where his mother still lived. He quickly fell back in with his old gang, working his way up in the Bloods chain of command and eventually taking charge of the Hempstead set.

"I knew how to run a business, and this ain't so different, really," he says. "This here beef we having [with the Crips] is like some corporate fight you'd read about in the *Wall Street Journal*, only this about our kind of business: rock cocaine."

For street dealers, there's still no more profitable drug than crack. A user can smoke as much of it as he wants, as opposed to powder, which limits him to the amount he's able to inhale before his nose goes numb or becomes too runny to continue. It takes a few minutes to feel the rush from powder cocaine, but crack vapor floods a user's lungs as soon as he inhales, delivering a quick, walloping high. Crack smokers describe the feeling as more intense than an orgasm, a wave of pleasure coursing through their entire bodies. In addition to being stronger than its powder alternative, crack is far cheaper—as little as $10 for a smokable rock, compared with $30 for a gram of powder.

Of course, crack has its drawbacks for the user. The drug's euphoric effects last only a few minutes, meaning a continuous supply is needed to keep the ride going. Even at $10 a rock, costs can add up quickly. If a user doesn't sustain his high, he can expect a wave of depression, anxiety, and irritability to wash over him. His cure, blessedly, is always just $10 away. And as he falls into an endless cycle of addiction, his dealer—often a Bloods or Crips member—gains a customer who can't live without his product.

"What you have here is a situation where both crews have a great product, and neither is open to being bought out," Ice says. "What you think's going to happen if neither side wants to give in? What happens is, things get messy. And that's what you seeing now. A whole lot of mess."

As the gang war carries over into February, police are seemingly powerless to stop it. Part of the blame lies in their inability to infiltrate either crew with undercover officers. Aside from developing an informant—a near-impossible task in the Triangle, with snitching punishable by death—an undercover operation is the only way the gangs' leaders can be taken off the streets in one fell swoop.

"It's a very difficult thing to do," says Hempstead chief of police Michael McGowan. "They've been successful thus far in keeping [undercovers] out."

The department's failure to infiltrate the crews isn't for lack of trying. At every house party where Bloods or Crips might be expected to congregate, police have tried to get undercovers inside. Each time, they've been thwarted.

"We know what cops look like, no matter what kind of gangster shit they try to dress up in," says Lamar Crawford. "A pig's a pig."

Another challenge facing law enforcement is the fact that there's no single agency with total responsibility for battling Hempstead's gangs. The

Nassau County Police Department, the county's biggest and best-funded law enforcement agency, has its own team of veteran gang investigators. But Hempstead is technically outside their jurisdiction, so while Nassau takes the lead on homicide investigations in the village, most other cases are assigned to the smaller, lesser-funded municipal force.

"We do what we can for them," says one Nassau detective involved in gang investigations. "But we have several dozen gangs we're dealing with across the county. It's a matter of priorities for us. There are only so many resources."

Both the Bloods and Crips exploited law enforcement's weaknesses in the years before the Triangle war, seeing just a handful of members arrested on major felony charges. As a result, once war broke out, both crews felt little need to scale back their drug enterprises or de-escalate the conflict.

"Way we see it, they ain't shit," Ice says, summing up his crew's opinion of the police. "Even if they do get their shit together long enough to make a case, ain't nobody out here going to talk to five-o or testify against any of us. That's just the code. That's law. That's the way it is . . . way it always will be."

Ice's characterization will prove accurate two nights later, when the protracted crackle of automatic gunfire echoes through the neighborhood just after eleven p.m. One explosive burst of ammunition. Then a second and third. Fifteen to twenty shots in all. Within minutes, police cars and ambulances are screeching up Linden Avenue, sirens blaring and lights flashing.

Near the stoop of a Crips stash house, a blood-soaked, Air Jordan sneaker lay in the road. Ten feet away lay a baby-faced Crips member, "Little James" Carter, with a quarter-size hole in his forehead. His other sneaker rests beside him in a rapidly expanding pool of blood. After the medical examiner takes James's body away, one of his fellow Crips, Savant Sharpe, picks up the pricey high-tops. Next day on the stoop, he's wearing them.

"No shame in this game," Savant says. "Besides, they too fresh to go in the garbage."

The investigation into James's murder follows a familiar pattern: Cops interview everyone in the area at the time of the killing; all claim to have seen nothing. As in most neighborhoods plagued by gang violence, the residents of Hempstead typically don't talk to police about gang shootings for fear they'll be the next targets. The "snitches get stitches" rule is taken seriously here, and those who break it can expect swift retribution, residents say.

"Why should I tell the cops anything?" says Donna Crawford, Lamar Crawford's aunt, who, after losing two sons to gang violence, refuses to talk to police about any crimes perpetrated by Bloods or Crips in the Triangle. "What are they going to do for me? Witness protection? Fly me to Hawaii? Walk my son home from school every day? I don't think so. I'll have to live here long after they're gone."

Donna's fears are shared by most people in the Triangle, who know police can't protect them or their families forever. Despite the neighborhood's code of silence, detectives investigating James's murder do everything in their power to catch his killer. They interview dozens of residents and gang members, pore over hundreds of hours of surveillance footage from area businesses, and prod street units to make a half-dozen or so drug arrests along MLK and the Triangle. The sweep, they hope, will lead someone to identify James's killer in exchange for a deal with prosecutors promising leniency.

But not one of the collared gangsters will talk.

"They think we're stupid, but we know Miranda," Steed says shortly after Ice posts his bail. He'd been charged with possession of cocaine, even though, he says, police found no drugs on him.

"That case is good as gone," he tells Ice. "They was just rounding niggas up and making up charges. No chance that shit sticks. We all know our rights and asked for lawyers."

Neither Steed nor any other gang members arrested in the wake of James's shooting prove useful to detectives, so they pursue other avenues. One of their most promising leads is a call made by an anonymous woman to a police tip line, claiming she'd overheard a Bloods member bragging he was about to "go shoot a Crip" the night of James's murder. The tipster even gave the plate number for a car she'd seen the man drive off in shortly before the shooting. Detectives comb through a Department of Motor Vehicles database and quickly identify the car, its registered owner, and his apartment number in a Hempstead project.

"Bingo," says Hempstead detective Mark Delahunt when the car owner's address pops up on his computer screen. "This has got to be our guy."

They rush to the man's apartment, believing they might be about to solve the case. But when they knock on the door and announce their presence, a hunchbacked old man with greasy gray hair and track marks on both arms opens it. He invites the detectives in and excuses himself to retrieve his dentures. An elderly woman emerges from a rear bedroom in her nightgown, offering the detectives coffee. After a few minutes of questioning, they determine that the old man's longtime girlfriend—a known crack addict, upset with him for taking back his nightie-clad ex—had exacted revenge by fingering him for James's shooting.

"Hell hath no fury like a crackhead scorned," Delahunt says after they leave the apartment. "This town is fucking unbelievable."

Three days later, a wake is held for Little James. His casket is ivory white and narrow, just wide enough to fit his body inside its purple velvet walls. He looks cramped in the open casket, but peaceful. A navy blue suit and oversize white dress shirt hide his chest wound. One mourner whispers that the bullet that killed him remains trapped inside his heart's left ventricle. Some Bloods snap pictures of James's corpse and post them on Facebook, accompanied by threats against the Crips.

James's little brother, Horace, tries to wake him up by prying open his eyes. When that doesn't work, he lowers his head and cries.

"Why I can't wake you?" the boy mumbles into the coffin. "Please wake up, James."

Tyrek doesn't attend the funeral, believing—correctly, it turns out—that police will be in attendance and leaning on people to snitch. But the day after James is buried, Tyrek makes his way to the graveyard to pay his respects. Standing over the mound of fresh dirt, he smokes one Newport after another, whispering prayers for James's soul.

"You a soldier, J, you a soldier," says Tyrek. "Please, God, let him be with you."

Tyrek looks exhausted, having slept just an hour or two since the shooting. He appears to have lost weight, too, his face gaunt and oily. He becomes defensive when asked if he feels any guilt for James's death—whether his murder is what's keeping him awake at night.

"I ain't the one who put the bullet in him," Tyrek says. "I didn't force him to work the corner. He asked me for work, so I put him to work. He was a good kid. But he'd grown up fast, too, so he wasn't really a kid no more, you know? He had drive . . . wanted to work, wanted to make some money so he could buy his own things and help out his mom and brothers."

From there, Tyrek offers a broader defense of his illicit activities in Hempstead, arguing they're the heart of the village's economic engine.

"I hear whispers in the hood, people saying I brought war to their blocks over a couple of corners. But the truth is, ninety-nine percent of these niggas around here would be jobless and making no money if I didn't do what I do in this community. Shit, who you think paid for church services, for the casket, for this plot right here?"

He points a finger at his own chest, tapping it emphatically.

"My money must not stink, 'cause ain't nobody turning it down."

After James's murder, Bloods involved in his shooting take precautions to try and ensure they're not arrested by cops or targeted by Crips. Doc Reed, the presumed triggerman, stays off the streets for six weeks. The police are looking to interview him, he knows, visiting his mother's house every day to ask whether he's turned up. So for the time being, he's living at the apartment of a Bloods associate in Brooklyn, along with Lamar, who'd overseen the drive-by mission. Doc and Lamar insist to their host that their intended target had been Dice Beckles, the Crip believed to have shot Doc in January.

"Nobody likes to see that type of collateral damage," Doc says of James's death. "But he chose sides; he wasn't there by accident. Little nigga been running with Tyrek's crew long as I can remember. You put yourself in that position, even if you a shorty, you know you ain't going to be immune. If you in it, you in it. Dice was the one who supposed to get hit. But he a little bitch, so he hit the deck when the shooting started. A soldier would've come out and met that shit head-on, instead of letting that young nigga die. Way I see it, James done fell because his own boy Dice was a fool. People on the block mad at our crew for killing the wrong Crip? Nah, that ain't logical."

Then Doc crystallizes the Bloods' mentality regarding the gang war.

"They started this shit, they can end it," he says of the Crips. "All they got to do is give up them corners in the Triangle."

CHAPTER THREE

Black Widows

Women always be making shit crazy.

—LAMAR

"Yo, Steed," Lamar says on a frigid February morning as they mix a batch of crack inside a Bloods cookhouse. "How you get that scar?"

"From fucking yo mama too hard," Steed says.

"How my mama going to give you a scar from fucking? That don't even make sense."

"Life don't make sense," Steed says with a shrug.

"For real," Lamar says. "How you get that?"

Steed ignores the question, adding more Arm & Hammer to the batch. He doesn't like to talk about the scar. In fact, none of the Bloods except Ice knows how he got it. They often see him stroking it, though, mostly when he's angry. It's a habit he's been trying to quit for years—a perceived weakness in a profession where weakness isn't allowed.

But Lamar won't let it go. He swears he won't tell a soul if Steed shares the story. He'll even finish up the cook on his own so Steed can go home early, he promises.

"From what I heard, you getting your scar had something to do with a girl," Lamar says. "A *fine*-ass girl."

"Yeah, that much I'll tell you is true," Steed says, remembering his nights with Patrice. "Girl was for real."

Stirring the batch, he reflects on that fateful, sun-drenched afternoon six years earlier when Tyrek showed up in his girlfriend's building lobby with a straight razor. They'd been beefing all year over Patrice Cunningham, one of the prettiest girls at Hempstead High School. Steed had spotted her first, winning her hand shortly after his mother moved their family from Los Angeles to Hempstead, wanting to get Steed away from the Southern California Bloods set he'd joined. Tyrek, already running with the Crips but not yet an official member, lived in the same building as Patrice and kept hitting on her, no matter how many times she insisted Steed was her man. The boys almost came to blows a few times over the situation, but Tyrek always backed down.

"See? He ain't nothing but a punk, Patrice," Steed said as they watched Tyrek slink off after one such encounter. "Ain't man enough for a girl like you."

Steed quickly forgot about the beef. Patrice got pregnant, and he was thrilled at the prospect of being a father. He planned to marry her once they graduated.

"You going to be a great dad," Patrice told him. "But you can't be running with no gang. I know you were Bloods in Cali, but that won't play here. Not if we're together. I need you to be down for me, not them."

"You got my word on that," Steed said. "No more banging."

But he hadn't accounted for Tyrek, who two months after getting punked in front of Patrice got offered official membership with the Crips. To prove his toughness, the Big Homies told him, he'd have to kill a Blood.

"I got one in mind," he said.

The following afternoon, Tyrek and a few Crips stood in the lobby of his and Patrice's building, knowing Steed walked her home from school each day. When the couple arrived, Tyrek pulled the blade from his backpack and lunged at Steed, who jumped backward just in time to avoid being gutted. Instead, as Tyrek swung the blade upward, it grazed Steed's chin, slicing it open where it met his right cheek.

But Tyrek wasn't finished. His momentum carried him forward until he stumbled into Patrice, the rusted blade piercing her swollen stomach.

Her skin made a tearing sound, "like paper ripping," Steed said, as the blade sliced through.

"Oomph," she cried as the Crips took off running.

"Oh my God, baby," Steed said. "Oh my God."

Steed ran upstairs to Patrice's parents' apartment and told them she'd been stabbed. Her mother called 911 while her father ran down with bathroom towels and tried to stem the blood gushing from his only child's stomach.

"What did you do?!" he howled at Steed.

The paramedics arrived and whisked Patrice away in an ambulance. Cops showed up a short time later and, at the direction of Patrice's father, handcuffed Steed.

"He stabbed my daughter," Gerald Cunningham said.

"I didn't, I swear," Steed said, and he was about to blurt out Tyrek's name when he noticed a crowd had assembled in the lobby. If he snitched, it would be even worse than going to jail for something he didn't do. His reputation in the neighborhood would be ruined, his punishment severe. So he held his tongue and spent the next few months in county lockup.

Patrice survived the stabbing, but her unborn child didn't. As soon as she was well enough to leave the hospital, Gerald Cunningham moved his family to LA, where, like Steed, they had roots.

As for Tyrek, the Crips Big Homies decided he'd sufficiently proven his toughness, despite his failure to kill Steed. They initiated him days after the stabbing and put him to work selling crack and weed. On Saturdays, he'd steal a car and drive a few Crips without felony convictions out to Virginia or Pennsylvania to buy guns and ammunition. They'd keep some of the guns for themselves and sell others on the street for double what they'd paid.

In his bedroom at night, Tyrek scratched out serial numbers and sawed off shotgun barrels in preparation for future missions. He moved quickly through the ranks, dropping out of Hempstead High School, getting a Crips gang sign tattooed across his chest, and gaining a reputation as a savvy, ruthless hustler who got things done. He was as adept at holding up liquor stores and bodegas as he was at clearing a Bloods corner with his fists or, if that failed, a submachine gun.

In those early years with the Crips, Tyrek would hang with fellow gang-sters in the crew's clubhouse or a Triangle stash house, getting blunted and drinking forties, always with the lights off so that any drive-by crews rolling past wouldn't have a clear target to aim for. For a teenager, he was afforded an unprecedented amount of responsibility, managing corner crews, carry-ing out assassinations, and mediating disagreements between fellow Crips. He was tough, smart, and creative in his schemes, his colleagues said, a gangland prodigy unlike any who'd come before him in Hempstead.

Once, when a stickup crew stole the bulk of a just-arrived cocaine package from the Crips, the Big Homies panicked, knowing they still owed their supplier for the full amount he'd fronted them. Tyrek, as usual, stayed calm. He convinced his crew to "step on" their remaining coke three times instead of once, thinning it out with powdered milk and Epsom salt so it would last longer. The dilution meant they could make up the lost profits by selling more crack of weaker strength. Some Crips worried their customers would complain and take their business to Bloods corners, but no one seemed to even notice the weakened crack. From then on, they stepped on all their product at the same rate, tripling profits.

When the set's leader, Nathan Dukes, was murdered in a shoot-out with Bloods in Brooklyn, Tyrek replaced him as Top Homie. Immedi-ately, he beefed up the gang's dealing operations, opening new Triangle corners and giving away free samples to junkies every morning to help spread buzz about Crips product. He and Tony routinely worked sixteen-hour days, cultivating a wider customer base and building up their reps. The Crips at that time sold only weed and weak, low-quality powder coke, which could be easily purchased from gang affiliates in the city. That changed after Tony got a line on a much stronger coke package being offered by a couple of Mexican boys he knew in Manhattan.

The Mexican coke, its sellers boasted, was "the ultimate in purity"—a product of far higher quality than most of the competing packages wending their way through Long Island and New York City markets at the time. The product's higher purity meant it could weather the crack-cooking process without losing its punch, so Tony convinced his Mexican contacts to front him half a kilo, or about $8,000 worth.

Next, he and Tyrek went to Walmart and put together a crack-cooking starter kit—Arm & Hammer baking soda, a saucer, glasses, and pans. They started cooking right away, breaking up their product into $20 hits of crack they called *ready rocks*, "since you could cook them up so fast and they was ready-made to smoke," Tony says. Within a few months, the Crips' Triangle crack-dealing operation was flourishing.

And it had all started with Tyrek giving Steed his scar—an attack that established Tyrek as a player in Hempstead's underworld and allowing for his rapid ascension through the Crips' ranks.

Four months after their encounter, Steed's lawyer pleaded the stabbing down from attempted murder to assault, for which he received time served and probation. Sprung from jail, he packed a bag and bought his own ticket back to LA, vowing to track down Patrice and make things right with her and her family.

He looked all over, scouring every LA neighborhood and waiting outside a different high school each day with hopes of spotting her. He kept this up week after week, month after month. To make a living, he did the only thing he thought himself qualified for: hooking up with a Bloods crew in South Central and dealing drugs. His reputation on the streets grew and promotions came quickly, until he was the set's co-leader. After five years of doing everything imaginable to find Patrice, he finally received a letter from her. "I forgive you. But please leave me be," she wrote. With that, Steed gave up, finally letting her go.

But there was another piece of unfinished business.

Tyrek, who Steed heard was now running the Hempstead Crips, still hadn't paid for the stabbing. So when Steed got a call from his old friend Ice, asking if he'd bring some of that good California coke out to Long Island, he decided to head back to Hempstead. The men teamed up to launch a thriving drug market along MLK, quickly moving in on Crips territory and setting the stage for the current Triangle war.

Steed hasn't yet gotten his revenge against Tyrek, but he believes his opportunity will come before the conflict is over. The only question, he says, is whether he can stay alive long enough to kill the man he says slayed his unborn child and drove away the woman he considers his "first love."

"Women always be making shit crazy," Lamar says. "Every nigga got a fucked-up story about women messing up their hustle. They can ruin your game real quick."

That's why Crips and Bloods are forbidden from discussing gang business with wives, girlfriends, or temporary pieces of ass, Lamar says. It's a rule the crews continually struggle with, despite the obvious risks.

"Just look at what happened to Rick," Lamar says.

"Who that?" asks Steed.

"Oh, you need to get schooled about Rick, yo."

In the mid-1990s, a Bloods dealer known as Fat Rick, despite moving slowly due to his 350-pound frame, turned the MLK projects into his own personal fiefdom. He's said to have earned several million dollars selling coke and heroin in the neighborhood, and, as his wealth grew, to have cultivated a harem of women—young, middle-aged, and old— scattered throughout Hempstead.

"Fat Rick was fucking five, six bitches a day, in addition to all the business he had to attend to," Lamar says. "The man was a legend in these parts. Larger than life. Fat Rick was like the Hempstead Biggie Smalls."

A popular parlor game in the projects at the time of Fat Rick's reign was guessing what might bring him down: the Crips, an STD, an angry boyfriend, or a heart attack caused by the stress from all those bedroom romps.

In fact, it was Rick's own compassion for a woman, his need to warn her of danger, that got him killed. The blame lay with one of his concubines, a long-limbed twenty-five-year-old hairdresser named Sheila who Rick sometimes slept with while her sanitation worker boyfriend made his rounds. In bed one afternoon, Rick casually mentioned to Sheila that she ought to stay away from the bodega across the street that night. A rival dealer, Carlos Slim, was to be assassinated there after ignoring multiple warnings to stop selling coke in Rick's territory. The hit would go down around ten p.m., when the dealer made his nightly visit to the bodega for cigarettes and Phillie blunts.

It was rare for Rick to reveal any details of his drug syndicate to women he bedded, but he made an exception for Sheila. He knew she stopped in the bodega some nights to buy Lotto tickets and didn't want her in harm's way when his hitter arrived. Sheila thanked Rick profusely for the heads-up.

But Sheila had also been sleeping with Carlos Slim, who rounded out her own male harem when Rick and her sanitation worker beau were otherwise occupied. As soon as Rick left her apartment, Sheila called Carlos and explained the plot. Instead of strolling into the bodega as usual that night, he and his crew staked out Rick's apartment building. When the big man arrived, they greeted him with a fatal volley from their .45s.

The lesson of Rick's demise hadn't been lost on Hempstead gangsters who followed in his footsteps.

"That's why you don't tell a ho anything—no exceptions," Lamar says. "No piece of pussy worthy dying or going to jail for. If it happened to Fat Rick, it can happen to anybody."

While forbidden from talking business with females, members of both crews still spend plenty of time with them. Young women from the Triangle and MLK walk down to the drug corners every day to try and cop for free, or at a discount, by flirting down dealer's prices. Some offer their bodies in exchange for drugs. Others promise to service the whole set. While leaders of both crews expressly forbid such exchanges, corner boys sometimes make them anyway.

Girlfriends, prospective girlfriends, and groupies are shooed away by the Crips during peak business hours, but tolerated when business is slow. The Bloods also allow women to hang around during lags in business. Bloods hustlers will sometimes sneak off with a project girl into an empty stairwell to trade a blow job or sex for a snort of coke or nugget of crack. Others take "lunch breaks" from their corners and head to their girlfriends' apartments for a half-hour of sex.

"Women are used and abused on these corners, the misogyny unparalleled," says Delahunt. "And yet they're pretty much all these gangsters think and talk about, outside of getting money and getting high."

Recently the gang war has kept most females off drug corners. Like other noncombatants, they fear catching a stray bullet. And some know they might be considered targets because of their relationship with the gangs. But while girlfriends and groupies keep their distance, Leticia Lewis, the only woman employed by either crew, does not.

Leticia—or "Black Widow," as she's known in the Triangle—is considered one of the best runners in the game. The secret to her success is simple: No police know she's part of the Crips drug operation. Rather, they believe she's just another "chicken head" who has sex with Crips corner boys or flirts her way into crack discounts. It's all part of her cover act, which she's developed with the guidance of her cousin, Tyrek. He put her to work a year earlier after a string of his male runners got locked up in rapid succession.

"Good help hard to find," Tyrek says. "She filled a void and filled it well."

To watch Leticia in action is to marvel at her ingenuity. She begins each workday by sashaying up to her designated corner in black high heels and kissing each hustler on his cheek, looking every bit the part of crew groupie or dope fiend. One of the corner boys will take her hand and lead her up to the stash apartment. Watching Leticia strutting off in her tight jeans, shiny heels, and puffy North Face jacket, an observer might assume she and her Crip companion are sneaking off for a quickie.

Inside the stash apartment, Leticia takes off her top. Taped to her midsection and breasts are several large bags packed with crack, fresh from a Bloods cookhouse. They're impossible to spot when she's wearing her North Face, even for veteran narcotics cops in the neighborhood.

"That was her idea, the extra large coat," Tyrek says. "She's a smart girl."

Leticia's delivery assignments vary. In the morning, it might be five g-packs[1] to the crew on Linden Place. Come lunchtime, it's three packs to the boys on Marvin Avenue and one to the Laurel Avenue crew. After each delivery, Leticia returns to a cookhouse or stash apartment to pick up more product and embark on another round of deliveries. Orders are made by corner supervisors based on how much product their crew is

---

[1] Packs of 100 crack vials sold for $10 apiece

selling on a given day. Each order must be approved by Tyrek or Tony, who can often be spotted doing what they call "crack math" on their iPhone calculators.

Leticia has an excellent memory, Tyrek says, so she never needs to take notes or make written calculations for her orders. Rather, she does all the math in her head. More remarkably, cops have never stopped her. Not once. For her efforts, Leticia makes between $300 and $400 a day, plus occasional bonuses paid by Tyrek.

But it's not just money that keeps her in the game.

"It's fun," she says. "You know, it's an adventurous life. I can't complain."

CHAPTER FOUR

Infantry

We're seen as less valuable to America, like we got nothing to contribute.
—TONY

Though runners like Leticia serve important roles in the Bloods and Crips, the most valuable members of both organizations—especially in wartime—are its "hitters," hit men who intimidate, strong-arm, and kill in accordance with the needs of their set's leadership. A hit man is rarely seen on a drug corner unless he's there to hurt someone, or worse. As a result, sightings of the men usually instill panic in all but their closest associates. Such fears are warranted; one look at them can mean the end for a rival dealer or indebted customer.

Each Hempstead crew has its own main hitter: The Crips have Joey "Rock" James; the Bloods have Jerome "Big Mac" McDaniel. Rock, for his part, has a reputation as one of the cruelest gangbangers in town. According to neighborhood lore, Rock cemented his legend in ninth grade at Hempstead High School after a neighborhood tough two grades ahead of him grabbed his big sister's bottom in the hallway. Sasha James began crying and ran off; her tormentor gave chase, continuing to squeeze her as she fled.

Rock, just walking out of social studies class, saw the kid molesting Sasha. He chased him down, held him by his collar, and palmed his head like a basketball in one of his massive hands. Then he bashed the persecutor's head against a nearby classroom door over and over until a crack opened down the middle of his forehead, "like a coconut," Rock says. The kid lay there until a teacher found him and called for paramedics, who arrived just in time to stem the bleeding and save his life.

Despite months of coaxing from school administrators and police, none of the students who had witnessed the beating would identify Rock as the perpetrator. A churchgoing loner who'd been easily ignored by classmates before the fight, Rock became a schoolhouse legend after it. Bullied peers, and sometimes their parents, sought him out for protection or to exact revenge for earlier beatings, robberies, and assorted humiliations they'd suffered. By the time Rock entered his sophomore year, both the Bloods and Crips had taken notice of his talents. Competition for potential recruits is fierce among the gangs, and Rock's skills—street smarts, intimidation, and toughness—are especially sought after.

In their efforts to recruit Rock, Hempstead Crips had a major advantage: He lived with his mother in a one-bedroom apartment on Linden Avenue, which sits squarely in Crips territory. The location of Rock's residence hadn't mattered to the gang until he'd carried out the legendary beatdown to protect his sister's honor. Few Crips could even recall ever seeing him in the neighborhood until word got around about his toughness.

"He had a face that blended in, like just a regular kid," says Flex Butler. "That's one of the things that made him so good. He didn't look like no killer or nothing. He looked like anybody you see around, so he snuck up on people real easy at first. But now? Everybody knows that nigga. His name ring out. So he's got to wear a mask when he go on missions."

Despite being at a geographical disadvantage, the Bloods tried luring Rock to their side first. As he walked out of school one afternoon, a car full of Bloods, including Doc and Ice, sat waiting for him at the curb.

"Yo, come here, shorty," someone in the car called out.

Rock was leery, knowing the boys were Bloods from MLK, and mortal enemies of Crips living on his block. But he approached the car anyway. Doc Reed reached out the passenger-side window and handed him an envelope.

"Open it," Doc said. Rock did and found $1,500 inside.

"That's for you, to use however you want," Doc said. "You could set your moms up in a bigger place. Buy yourself some new clothes. And when you done spending that, there's more."

Stunned by the gift, Rock asked what he had to do in return, figuring he was being hired to protect or beat someone—although he couldn't imagine why the Bloods would need his help.

"My nigga, we want you in red," Ice said from the backseat. "We want you riding with us."

They drove him to a Bloods associate's house off MLK that doubled as an occasional party spot for the crew. There, they smoked blunts packed with their finest weed, getting Rock so high he could barely stand up to leave once it was time to go home. That night, he slept with the envelope of cash under his mattress, wondering whether he should give it to his mom to get a nicer place, or give the money back and decline the membership offer. He knew the danger in accepting Bloods money and membership while still living on Crips turf, but figured he and his mom could quickly move to a new apartment outside enemy territory.

By the time school ended the next day, he'd decided on accepting the cash. But as the Bloods waited for him at the curb again, some Crips Big Homies intercepted him at the schoolhouse door. It turned out they had something to offer that Rock wanted even more than money and a new apartment.

He was a virgin until that night, when the Crips got him high and brought him to the home of a forty-something crack queen who, despite her addiction, still had her looks. She slept with him as part of a deal she'd worked out with the crew for some free vials. Rock spent the whole weekend holed up at her place, and when school started again on Monday, he was working a Crips corner instead of in class. Two months later, his membership was official.

"Shit was meant to be," Rock says. "Allegiances born lots of different ways in the Triangle."

For his first assignment, Tyrek tasked Rock with debt collection. When force was needed, the new Crip used it expertly. But street enforcement called for nothing more than intimidation and brutality, a far cry from killing with guns. For that, Rock needed training. So, every Wednesday, Tyrek and Tony drove him out to an isolated stretch of woodland in southern Nassau County. There, they fired at beer bottles and paper targets they posted on trees, shooting hundreds of rounds of ammo. Rock honed his aim with nine-millimeter Walthers and Glocks, a .38 Smith & Wesson, a Cobra .380, a Remington pump-action shotgun, and even a Desert Eagle .44 Magnum, a famously high-powered gun capable of blowing an enemy gangster's head clean off with one shot. By summer's end, he was routinely hitting bull's-eyes with them all.

Today, his marksmanship is beyond expert. By Tyrek's estimate, Rock's "body count"—the number of people he's killed, alone or with the help of others—is likely between ten and fifteen. But Tyrek refuses to waste the talents of his best hitter on routine drive-bys any Crip "with decent aim and a little heart" could pull off. Sounding every bit the CEO, Tyrek says he's waiting for the "right opportunity to utilize Rock's skill set."

In the meantime, Rock imparts wisdom to younger Crips who aren't as handy with their firearms. Like the woodland target practice his bosses once gave him, Rock stages drills for young gangsters aimed at honing their aim and tactical skills. In one drill, they carry paintball guns and try to clear the wooded area of "combatants"—Crips wearing red, playing the role of Bloods. The "enemy" gangsters leap out from behind trees, taking aim with paintball guns of their own. One gang member serves as a referee, shouting "Out!" whenever a combatant is struck. Those who make it through the drill alive win an extra day's wages and—if Rock is especially impressed with their performance—a free half-hour with one of the prostitutes who turns tricks in the gang's territory.

The Bloods, too, stepped up training at the direction of Big Mac. As the Hempstead set's primary hitter, he's tasked with making sure gang members are proficient with their guns. Thanks to him, all Bloods know how to properly clean, oil, and assemble their weapons. Before he began schooling them, their guns would sometimes jam or fall apart in the middle of shoot-outs, their clips sliding out at crucial moments.

"That don't happen anymore," Mac says. "Shit was embarrassing."

He also moonlights as a security guard for a famous R & B singer but he says the money he makes as part of Ice's drug-dealing operation is more than he'd make working full-time in the performer's detail.

"Once you get used to money like this with [the Bloods], you can't go back to waiting on paychecks week to week."

A barrel-chested, weight-lifting enthusiast with a glistening bald head, Mac's a stickler for detail, and hard on gang members under his command. He disciplines them harshly for infractions like showing up late for work, needlessly flashing their guns in public, or stealing from the gang. Early in the Triangle war, a Bloods foot soldier accidentally fired a bullet through his next-door neighbor's wall, blowing a young boy's ear off. After the child's mother complained to Bloods leaders, Mac paid a visit to the offending gangster, beating him so badly he promised never to switch the safety off again.

"Nigga, you know you can't be playing with that gun like a toy," Mac said after the beatdown, the kid leering at him through two black eyes. "That's your penalty. Don't be messing with your piece."

The most severe punishments, though, are reserved for gang members caught skimming drug proceeds or product. When a seventeen-year-old Bloods dealer named Derek "Big Boy" Owens began cutting his corner crew's coke more heavily in order to stretch their supply further and keep the extra cash for himself, several pipeheads—a term reserved for Hempstead's most hard-core crack addicts—noticed the difference in strength. They reported the weakened product to Doc, who's in charge of quality control for the Bloods. He dispatched Mac to fix the situation, which the hitter did by docking Big Boy two weeks' wages and punching the beefy teenager in his belly until he coughed up blood.

"One thing you never do is steal from your own people," Mac told Big Boy as he lay writhing on the ground. "That's your penalty."

Two months later, Big Boy would go a long way toward earning back the trust of his bosses by winning three consecutive tactical drills—a new Bloods record.

"We Baghdad-ready," Big Boy bragged. "Those niggas in the Triangle ain't nothing to us after the training we done."

Despite his occasional cruelty, Mac is proud of his pupils when they perform well. Some even see him as a father figure in a neighborhood desperately in need of one. The irony of those boys viewing him in a paternal light, despite the violence he routinely perpetrates against them, isn't lost on Mac.

"It's a fucked-up thing, but the truth is, a lot of these niggas don't have nobody who gives a damn about them," Mac says one day as he and a few Bloods are leaving a gang associate's home in Rockaway Beach, Queens. "I guess I do care about these younger niggas. But I'm just doing my job, man."

Risks, he knows, are also part of his job. For that reason, he's nearly always on alert for enemy gangsters who might seek revenge. But for a moment this afternoon, breathing in the cool beach air blowing in off the ocean, Mac lets his guard down. He's reaching into his pocket for his car keys when a well-built man wearing a black ski mask walks up from behind and presses a gun to his neck.

Outside the home, a single gunshot rings out. Several of Mac's fellow gangsters run outside to find him laying in the yard. His neck's been torn open by the shot and he's moaning loudly, rolling around on the grass. His wallet falls from his back

Pictured here, one of the masks Rock uses when he goes on missions. The Crips hitter says he must hide his face when committing certain crimes because he is well-known in the neighborhood and would otherwise be easily recognized.
KEVIN DEUTSCH

pocket,opening to reveal a photo of his smiling daughter in a school uniform, her image now splashed with blood.

A blue Ford Taurus double-parked across the street screeches off, the masked gunman visible in the passenger seat. The Bloods draw their weapons and level them at the fleeing car. This reporter ducks back inside just as they begin emptying their clips in the Ford's direction, shooting out a taillight as the sound of the car's groaning engine fades into the distance.

The Bloods are heard yelling outside, screaming at each other to lift Mac into a car and get him to the hospital. Their vehicles roar off.

The next day, Ice explains that the shot to Mac's neck was fatal. "I don't know which of them stupid-ass niggas did this," Ice says. "But somebody got to pay."

At Queens Medical Center, doctors had tried frantically to save Mac once his gang brothers dropped him off. Dr. Jonathan Rose, the physician who'd pronounced Mac dead, said a short prayer for the fallen twenty-two-year-old hitter, noted the time of death, and lingered an extra few moments with the body. It turned out he'd seen the murdered patient before.

"He came in about a year ago with a bullet in his leg, and maybe two, three months before that, with a graze wound," says Dr. Rose, whose patient lists some nights read like a Bloods–Crips membership roster. "I remember him because, both times he was here, he was the sweetest kid. I mean, tough guy, definitely. He looked like a hard-ass, and probably shot any number of people. But he was a real nice kid to me.

"First time I treated him, he asked me all about my daughters . . . said he had one himself. Second time he came in, he remembered my little girls' names and asked how they were. Bright kid, too. I remember I told him, 'Get out of this life while you can. Because when you live by the sword, you die by the sword.' I thought maybe I got through to him. But then I saw him tonight. And I thought to myself, 'Damn, he didn't listen.'"

For the Bloods, the vital questions of who shot Mac and why aren't easily answered. Because the gunman wore a mask during the attack, no one's able to identify him. And the list of potential Crips suspects is end-less. Mac accumulated too many enemies to count in his role as top Bloods hitter and enforcer, leaving several sons fatherless and half a dozen enemy gangsters either wheelchair-bound or hauling around oxygen machines.

In such a world—"a suburban jungle," as Mac often called Hemp-stead—normal rules don't apply. The Triangle is not truly a part of the affluent region that circles it; it's a neighborhood cast aside, with its own bosses and martyrs, language and codes, a suburban war zone seemingly abandoned by its wealthier Long Island neighbors. In such a world, the death of a man like Mac—a "stone killer," as Detective Delahunt called him—is neither unusual nor unexpected. The soldiers on this battlefield all know they must live by the sword. And all are prepared to die by it.

"They're willing to risk their lives on those corners every day, because the money is so good," Delahunt says. "There aren't many other ways for them to make this kind of a living around here."

⌒

In a village where unemployment is 16 percent—the highest on Long Island—Hempstead Crips and Bloods have built an economic system firing on all cylinders, twenty-four hours a day, seven days a week. In a community where 21 percent of residents live below the poverty line, nearly twice the state average, a drug corner is the rare local business that generates large cash profits day after day, a thriving enterprise immune from outside market forces and economic uncertainty. It's a system so successful that its participants risk just about everything—their freedom, their families, their lives—to be part of it.

The drug markets offer steady work and same-day pay. For young men unable to find legitimate jobs because of their criminal records or lack of education and job skills, the corners also offer validation, respon-sibility, and respect. If there's no room for them in the job market outside the Triangle, there's plenty of room within it: opportunities to move up, to get rich, to get women, and to find a niche where before, none was appar-ent. If their lives lack meaning and purpose outside their gangs' territories, they're plainly meaningful and purposeful within them. These hustlers are, after all, the essential human capital keeping the drug markets humming. Here, slinging vials and hiding stashes, young men with no obvious place in America's legitimate economy find that they belong, that they're significant, that they matter. For the first time in their lives, they are defined by their *work*. And they've found out it feels pretty good.

"Way I see it, this is what I'm meant to be doing," Tyrek says. "I'm an entrepreneur."

In this ten-block-long world of the Triangle and MLK—the only world these young men know—hustlers say they see no opportunity outside their own neighborhoods; the desperate inheritances of poverty and lack of education passed down to their parents have also passed to them. It's a world of stoicism and hardness, where gangsters boast about how much prison time they can do without breaking, and how willing they are to die for their set.

It's a world where the preservation of one's masculinity means everything, for weakness of any kind is considered a dangerous liability. And it's a world where most any type of violence—against women, children, and senior citizens—can be justified through twisted gangland logic.

In this world, petty feuds wipe out multiple generations of the same families. Acts of brutality are seen as righteous, because they're conducted in accordance with the unwritten Laws of the Street. As for police, gang members see them as enemy forces patrolling their neighborhoods not to protect and serve, but to persecute and destroy. Their hatred of law enforcement is perhaps the one thing that unites Crips and Bloods, who, like Steed, would rather go to jail than snitch to cops, even about their mortal enemies.

In such a world, new horrors lay around every corner. Clothing stores sell memorial T-shirts with a space left blank for the victim's face. Grieving families simply bring in a photograph of the fallen Blood or Crip and—for $30—his likeness is quickly silk-screened onto the shirt. In this world, gang names are spray-painted on walls, and shrines to the murdered, featuring Hennessy bottles, shell casings, and condolence cards, are created with numbing frequency.

In this world, friends of the dead tattoo their brethren's names on their chests and arms, so that they're constantly reminded of the need to

Makeshift memorials for murder victims, like the one pictured here, are erected with numbing frequency in the Triangle.
KEVIN DEUTSCH

avenge. Gang members even build RIP Facebook pages for themselves while still alive, knowing they're more likely than not to die prematurely.

"I know what's coming; we all know," says Steed, who has completed his own online memorial page. "Ain't none of us delusional. But you can't dwell on that stuff. You got to live while you're here."

The rules of this world are different, too. Here, the death of an innocent from a stray bullet is seen as the cost of doing business and the absence of community cooperation with police that follows, inevitable. Here, guns and knives are the answer to most any problem, and gangsters who survive long enough to have kids become fathers much like their own: rarely home, in and out of prison, heirs to a cruel legacy that's turned murder, drug dealing, gunshot wounds, and incarceration into coming-of-age traditions in the Triangle. More than 1.7 million kids in the United States had a parent in prison as of 2007, according to federal and state prison data. In the Triangle, where roughly one out of every three males serves time behind bars, having at least one close relative in prison is almost expected. Despite all the suffering endured by their parents, almost no one who enters the drug business here leaves it of his own accord. The gangsters say that's because most of them have felony records, leaving almost no alternatives to make a real living outside the drug rackets.

"We're seen as less valuable to America, like we got nothing to contribute," Tony says. "So why not sell drugs if that's how the world feel about you? Why not make money the best way you can, given everybody already done gave up on you? We're America's leftovers, for real. They don't need us, and they don't know what to do with us. That's why we out here hustling."

Without traditional accomplishments to take pride in, like diplomas and varsity letters, Hempstead Crips and Bloods brag instead of their moneymaking prowess and willingness to kill. Without any real sense of civic pride, they name-check the nearest highway exits, zip codes, and street names. With no authentic outlets for their intelligence or creativity, they invent words and universes all their own. Westbury, a neighborhood in Nassau, becomes "Westbloodbury." Nassau's area code, 516, becomes a battle cry.

"Hempstead, exit thirty-two and twenty-one, LI, Parkside to Park Ave. That's Crip money, nigga," boasts one Hempstead Crip in a video his set made and posted online, seeking what they call "street fame."

"Blue money, blue world. That's Long Island money right there. Blue island, niggas. Wild stylin,' five-one-six."

Despite all their bravado, most Bloods and Crips aren't blind to the inevitability of their failure. They know that whatever success they find in the Triangle and other drug markets will be fleeting—that at some point in the coming months, their corner escapade will almost certainly be over. When it ends, they'll either be dead, like Little James and Mac; wheelchair-bound from a bullet, like Savant Sharpe's older brother, Nico, a former Crips enforcer; or in jail, awaiting a long prison sentence, like most every Crips Big Homie of the past thirty years.

Even as they play at being invincible, the gangsters carry the secret of their own demise. Yet they continue down the path toward ruin, their desire to belong, receive respect, and get rich outweighing their hopes to one day escape the ghetto, to go further than their parents. Money may lure them to the corners, but it's the feeling that their lives finally have purpose that keeps them there.

"This is what God put me on Earth to do, or else I wouldn't be here," says Rock, kissing the gold crucifix he wears around his neck.

The worst part, Delahunt says, is that the Triangle conflict "is just one of hundreds being fought by Bloods and Crips sets throughout the country. These young men are at war, not in Iraq or Afghanistan, but in our own cities and suburbs. It seems like nobody realizes that—either that, or no one cares."

Dr. Rose, too, has seen the human toll of these gang wars. In all the hospitals he's worked in across America, from San Diego to West Palm Beach, he's treated Bloods and Crips who kill and maim each other in droves. In emergency rooms from Chicago to Atlanta, he's seen gangsters wheeled in after getting shot by childhood friends over gang allegiances, perceived disrespect, or, sometimes, just for the hell of it.

"Too many kids have died in front of me over these stupid Bloods–Crips beefs," Rose says. "When will people wake up and see these are actual wars being fought under our noses, in our own suburbs, in *Long Island*, for chrissake? And when will the gang members see the waste of it all?"

Rock, for one, says he's too caught up in the local celebrity his reputation affords him to think about whether he's wasting his life, or about the likelihood he'll die a violent death. When he goes out to pick up his car from the shop two days after Mac's murder, he admits to this reporter he'd been the masked gunman who cut Mac down. Still, he says, the possibility of retribution doesn't occur to him. He'd taken care to hide his face, after all, and knows the Bloods must be in the dark about who did the shooting.

"I'm too smart for those slobs," Rock says, using a derogatory term for Bloods. "I got more important things to think about, anyway. Like my ride."

He's been waiting on a call about his new car, a navy blue Mercedes E-Class, from the mechanics over at the Mercedes service center on Graham Avenue, half a block from the Triangle. The car's been in the shop ten days now, and Rock says he's tired of the delay. He wants to show it off to the girls in the neighborhood tonight, maybe find himself a date.

"When I roll past in my E-Class, they ain't going to be able to resist getting in," Rock says. "That car's an aphrodisiac, yo."

Mercedes, to the surprise of many, built their local service center at the edge of a notorious drug market; the affordable rent and tax breaks were apparently enough to allay any concerns over customer safety. Its construction was part of Hempstead's revitalization effort—an attempt to attract new businesses and rehabilitate its image as an unsafe suburb in decline. Local politicians believed having a luxury brand in town might help to improve the village's reputation and perhaps attract other prestige companies. But the Crips and Bloods, seeing those expensive cars rolling past the Triangle every day, had other ideas.

At first, Crips approached Mercedes owners outside the service center and touted their powder cocaine, which they market mostly to well-off white customers. The drivers looked terrified when gangsters approached, speeding past a stop sign that called for them to stop in Crips territory. Indignant Mercedes customers complained about the swarms of over-zealous dealers harassing them every time they got an oil change. Within a few months of the center's opening, municipal workers removed the stop sign, allowing panicky drivers to flee the area as quickly as possible.

"This is one of the only spots where you can see the idea of the suburban Long Island dream of money, luxury, and success butting up against the reality that is the crack and gang culture," Delahunt says. "Here, all illusions are lost."

Having a Mercedes branch within view of their corners caused many Crips to covet the cars. After all, the vehicles represent everything the gangsters grew up without: luxury, excess, privilege, and power. Rock was the first to give in and buy one with his drug-sale proceeds. Despite the car's hefty price tag, it was trouble from the start, stalling at stoplights and failing to switch gears as fluidly as Rock expected for a luxury ride. At the service center, he's making his displeasure known to the mechanic, demanding the repairs be made immediately—and without costs.

"How y'all going to charge me that kind of money and give me a faulty product?" he says. "In my line of work, you get killed for doing that."

The mechanic looks up from under the hood, eyebrows raised, perhaps interpreting Rock's bluster as a threat. He mutters something about how he's "not going to be threatened by some fucking drug dealer" and stalks off, returning a few minutes later accompanied by a service center manager. That man orders Rock to leave the premises at once.

"Fuck y'all racist mothafuckas," he says, climbing into his $50,000 lemon and heading back to the Triangle. "Luxury, my ass. This why Long Island be tripping, man."

When he gets to the Crips' clubhouse, his fellow gangsters are staring intently at the TV, the volume turned way up. It's the afternoon news. An unidentified man has been shot and killed five miles away in Freeport, the newscaster says. No arrests have been made.

"They got Crazy Ray," Tyrek tells Rock.

Crazy Ray was a Crips dealer responsible for running a busy drug corner in Freeport. Ray had nothing to do with Mac's murder, but he found himself in the wrong place at the wrong time when the Bloods rolled out, looking for revenge.

"Damn," Rock says. "This a fucked-up day."

"It's just war, nigga," Tyrek says. "Ain't no thang."

CHAPTER FIVE

The Cost

*Crack was the atomic bomb of the ghetto. And the scariest part was,
any fool could build that bomb.*

—MARCUS JACKSON

At forty-five years old and counting, the nationwide Bloods-Crips conflict has gone on longer than any war in the history of the United States. It's claimed approximately 20,000 lives,[1] most of them young black men involved in the drug trade or other criminal enterprises, but also many innocents: little boys and girls caught in gang crossfire; mothers, fathers, and grandparents cut down by stray bullets; and members of law enforcement murdered while serving their communities.

More than 6,500 US troops died in America's wars in Iraq and Afghanistan between 2001 and 2013. In that time, at least 6,700 Americans were killed in violence linked to Bloods and Crips sets in 37 states. More than 10,000 others were wounded. The Triangle war is but one of the (at least) 425 violent Bloods-Crips conflicts happening at any given time across the country. And it's not just cities playing host to these deadly feuds. Rather, America's suburbs are increasingly serving as battlefields for Crips and Bloods, attracting more warring sets as gang leaders seek unclaimed suburban drug corners and gentrification prices poor minority families out of cities.

---

[1] Statistics in this chapter are drawn from the author's analysis of police and court records; local, state, and federal government data on gunshot injuries in all fifty states; thousands of newspaper and magazine articles; and his interviews with more than 250 Bloods, Crips, and gang investigators.

Although the wars these gangsters fight over territory, debts, girls, and petty sleights are worlds apart from the ones fought overseas, the end results—death and destruction—are the same. And when one factors in the damage these gang battles inflict on hundreds of American communities, their domestic impact may in fact be worse.

"You know that scene in *Forrest Gump* where they flash back and you see all of Lieutenant Dan's male relatives dying in war after war after war? Well, you could have made the same scene about my family when it comes to being in the Crips, except they'd be falling down on drug corners," says Donta Chambliss, a former Hempstead Crip who served fifteen years in prison for dealing crack. "My dad was a Crip. My dad's brother was a Crip. My brother was a Crip. My cousin was a Crip. And you know what? Every one of them is dead because of gangbanging. That ain't no movie. That's New York."

Despite more than four decades of ceaseless carnage among Bloods and Crips, most Americans have ignored the nationwide gang war. One reason for that, victims of gang violence say, is that so little of the bloodletting visited upon black communities has spilled over into white ones. But with long-standing city drug markets becoming oversaturated and urban gentrification pushing more minorities into the suburbs, including Long Island, that dynamic is beginning to change.

"All you have to do is sit in the ER of a Nassau County or Westchester hospital to see the cost of this war in human terms in the suburbs," Dr. Rose says. "People need to wake up to the fact that drug dealers . . . are looking for that same suburban money and success that brings everyone else here."

"These are wide-open markets," says Delahunt. "And so the suburbs are becoming their new battlefield."

Despite an ever-growing list of casualties, there are no combat histories written about the people killed, raped, and grievously wounded in this conflict, no tomes chronicling this war's battles or the psychic toll they've taken. As a result, it's difficult to determine how a single gang dispute managed to poison so many communities, or understand how it has endured despite intensive efforts from law enforcement.

It is, however, fairly clear where and when the whole thing started: Watts, Los Angeles, 1969.

Four years after the 1965 Watts riots—six days of violent, racially driven unrest that killed 34 people, left more than 1,000 injured, and destroyed or damaged hundreds of buildings—a group of Japanese senior citizens walking home from a community meeting were approached by a group of young black men in the battle-scarred neighborhood. Some of the teens grabbed the women's purses and ran off—a crime that seemed minor at the time, but would become part of gangland lore.

The purse-snatchers were a nameless crew, a gang of toughs who committed petty crimes and protected their turf from other cliques. Bad as they were, the boys were not yet an organized, self-identified street gang. They got their name thanks to one of the victimized Japanese women, whose poor English led her to identify her assailant as "a crip. A crip with a stick," according to *Do or Die*, Leon Bing's book about Bloods and Crips in LA. The old woman was trying to say one of her assailant's had a bad leg and was "crippled," using a stick to help him walk. A reporter at the police station overheard the "crip" description and mentioned it in a story, according to Bing's account. The name stuck.

That same group of roving troublemakers, now known as Crips, kept robbing and beating people, expanding their territory and gaining affiliate groups. Young men in LA who felt threatened by the bourgeoning Crips crews organized their own gang. They called themselves the Pirus, after Pine Street, where many of them lived.

In Watts, Crips took to wearing blue bandanas to identify themselves. The Pirus, rapidly becoming the Crips' main competitors for members and turf, liked the idea, and adopted red kerchiefs as their hallmark. Around the same time, they started calling themselves Bloods,[2] which is what African-American troops in Vietnam called each other. The gang members, now accustomed to committing acts of violence, identified

---

[2] Many Bloods sets still prefer to be called Pirus.

more with their war-hardened counterparts in the military than with noncombatants in their own neighborhoods.

"The black vets who served in 'Nam were the baddest mothafuckas around. And we thought we were the baddest niggas in our neighborhood," says Reginald Franks, sixty-two, an early Bloods member in LA who now lives on Long Island. "So we said, 'That's the perfect name for us. Bloods.' We saw ourselves as an army. Crips and Bloods sets today still have that soldier mentality."

The gangs were an immediate sensation in the housing projects of Watts and Compton, where antipolice sentiment had hardened in the post-riot years. Young men clamored to join, wanting the prestige and protection that came with being part of a cold-blooded crew in a dangerous part of town. Word of the gangs spread to projects throughout the city, inspiring other Angelenos to form their own sets.

In a few months' time, there were dozens of Crips and Bloods sets throughout LA.

With more sets came more territorial disputes, leading to brawls, shootings, and other retaliatory violence between Crips and Bloods throughout the 1970s. Those crimes, in turn, led to prison sentences for an increasing number of gang members.

Behind bars, their gang allegiances depened. They stuck together for protection from each other, as well as from Hispanic gangs, white power groups, and other crews linked by ethnicity, religion, or politics. In California's vast and violent corrections system, the reputation of the Bloods and Crips grew. And the war fought between them on the streets of LA extended beyond prison walls. "If you couldn't get at somebody outside, you sure as hell knew who was Blood or Crip on the inside, and could hit back there," Franks says. "The war outside the jails and prisons became one and the same with the one [taking place] inside them. There weren't any lines drawn. War was war just the same, and it was ugly."

Many gang members, convicted under strident federal drug laws enacted in the mid-1980s, were also sent to federal prisons scattered throughout the country. They brought with them the same hatred of the enemy as their counterparts on the streets and in state prisons, beating the drums of war in far-flung detention facilities where, just a few years earlier, no one had even heard of the Bloods and Crips.

"The gangs spread like a disease," says Marcus Jackson, sixty-four, a member of one of the early Crips sets in Watts. "I know, because I was a carrier of that disease. I carried it from prison to prison, just like a lot of us did. The battle went on wherever you went—no exceptions. The line between banging on the inside and the outside became invisible."

Over time, both gangs' prison networks grew more organized, with rigid command structures and various means of receiving information from the streets—including through prison guards, who were themselves affiliated with one gang or the other. Membership grew exponentially. And when new inductees were released, they carried their beefs and chest-thumping rhetoric back to their hometowns, starting new sets, waging new battles.

Back in LA, the top-down hierarchy and disciplined approach of the original Crips and Bloods sets led to the drawing of firm territorial lines, making entire neighborhoods no-go zones for enemy crews. Gang violence in parts of the city was bad in the late 1970s, but it was about to get worse. For into this violent universe an explosive new element, rock cocaine, was introduced.

"Crack was the atomic bomb of the ghetto," Jackson says. "And the scariest part was, *any* fool could build that bomb."

With the crack economy thriving in the 1980s, Bloods and Crips morphed into something more than youth street gangs. They became ruthless, business-savvy, drug-trafficking confederations—violent entrepreneurs who married their gangs' structural hierarchies to the cocaine trade. Some of their leaders became millionaires. Most gang members gave up working legitimate jobs, if they had them, to toil full-time for their crews. They filled the same positions—dealer, runner, lookout, and tout—that make up today's drug gangs.

With hundreds of millions of dollars up for grabs in the crack trade, violence already engrained in the Bloods–Crips conflict spiraled further out of control. The gangs became criminal insurgents, taking over entire neighborhoods, daring police and law-abiding citizens to stop them.

Bloods and Crips branched out to other states, setting up new markets with supply lines running back to California. It marked the beginning of a massive cross-country migration by the Crips and, later, the Bloods, which would see the gangs open scores of drug corners coast to coast in nearly every state by the mid-1980s.

In this way, a single gang dispute over neighborhood turf lines escalated into a series of shooting wars fought over drug territory, leading to hundreds of murders each year across the country.

"At first, we were just fighting for territory, because it was kind of an 'our neighborhood is harder than yours' type of thing," Franks says. "Once crack showed up, it was like . . . the stakes went up in a way you can't even measure. It was a gold rush. Everyone wanted crack, and once they tried it, they couldn't stop smoking it. Us and the Crips were making piles of money. We were like gold prospectors, only we dealt in death. Crack was death. Everybody knew it, but that didn't matter, because there was finally a way to make money in places where you couldn't make any before."

Crack democratized cocaine not just for users, but for dealers as well. It didn't take a large investment anymore for a lowly corner boy to become a real player. He could buy $150 worth of powder coke, cook it into crack, and come away with enough rocks to sell $1,500 worth. Those rocks would be more powerful than their powder precursor because of the higher concentration of cocaine and could multiply a dealer's original investment by ten times. It was every hustler's dream: a more addictive product that could be turned into more money.

The government intensified its War on Drugs in response to the explosion in crack dealing, forming elite federal drug task forces and exponentially boosting local law enforcement funding to fight traffickers, but their actions did little to slow the expansion of the Bloods and Crips into new markets. As police and federal agents cracked down on drug sales, mostly in black neighborhoods, tens of thousands of black men involved in the crack trade were imprisoned, their families left without breadwinners or a viable source of income. And with the advent of mandatory minimum sentencing laws, crack dealers were treated much more harshly than those who sold powder cocaine and other drugs. Eighteen-year-old touts caught selling a pocket full of crack routinely got fifteen to twenty years in prison, while runners caught carrying larger amounts sometimes received life sentences.

Because crack dealing was concentrated in black neighborhoods, the sentencing guidelines often had the effect of treating African-American crack dealers differently from any other class of criminal. A heroin dealer convicted on federal charges of selling that highly addictive opiate in New York City would be sentenced to a fraction of the prison time of a hustler selling rocks on the same block—disparate treatment that embittered a generation of blacks.

To make matters worse, harsh penalties for crack dealing did little to dissuade dealers and users. Police would arrest an entire corner crew, only to return a few days later and find new dealers in their place. When they busted *that* crew, another one replaced them. The most popular law enforcement strategies of the 1980s and '90s—arresting street-level dealers while seizing as much coke, weed, and heroin as possible—curbed neither the demand for narcotics nor the willingness of Crips and Bloods to sell them. America's prison population swelled into the world's largest, due in part to the mass incarceration of drug offenders.

"The crack sold by the Bloods and Crips was destroying families and communities, but so were the mandatory minimum laws," says Delahunt. "Most of the people getting long prison terms weren't the gang leaders. Instead, they were the lowliest guys in the crew: messengers, touts, people like that. Because the real hustlers, the real merchants of death, stayed off the streets."

The unfairness of mandatory minimum drug laws and their damage to African-American communities was clear, but it took the US Justice Department until 2010 to start rolling them back. That year, Congress reduced the 100-to-1 disparity between sentences for crack versus powder coke offenses. In 2014, Democrats and Republicans began work on a bipartisan sentencing overhaul bill, with the goal of ending mandatory minimums for low-level drug offenses, following the lead of a number of states where crack-related sentencing reforms have been enacted.

Today, drug laws are being revised to read much the way they did before crack's arrival in America. What hasn't changed is the demand for the drug in poor, gang-plagued neighborhoods like the Triangle.

"They're changing the laws, because the laws are unfair, but the problem is that crack is still everywhere, from the Triangle to Compton to Connecticut," says Jackson, who now works as an addiction counselor. "And in some places, it's as big as ever. The government essentially gave up on all these neighborhoods, because they couldn't find a better way to beat the dealers than to lock up all the young players, which didn't fix a thing. But look where we are now: right back where we started, the only difference being there are a lot more drugs than just crack tearing down communities these days. At the end of the drug war, the result is most definitely not muddled. The dealers won."

In Hempstead, that opinion is one of the few things Bloods and Crips agree on.

"We already won," Tyrek says, declaring victory in the War on Drugs. "Ain't nobody about to stop the slinging. When people talk about the war, I say, 'If you all fighting a war against what we doing out here, than you ain't too good at your job,' because hustlers still grinding in every single hood. Shit, they grinding in every suburb."

Some gang members in the Triangle—as well as members of Bloods and Crips sets in Manhattan, Brooklyn, and Queens—say their crews are emboldened by recent sentencing reforms. Having once feared life sentences for crack-related convictions, they now sling with the knowledge that any arrest will lead to considerably less prison time, if any, than what they'd have once faced. Accordingly, the gangsters wholeheartedly endorse the changes.

"It's a good idea to change the laws, because crack ain't any worse than powder," says Tyrek. "Why do I go to jail ten or fifteen years longer than the white boy who gets caught snorting powder? Way I see it, with these changes, I can do what I do now without having to always be worried about going away for life behind some bullshit laws. Now, fair is fair. So it's a positive for me and my people. We a little more relaxed. And real [money] coming in on the regular."

Just as it has since its arrival in America some thirty-five years ago, crack continues to destroy the social fabric of communities where it's sold. Government data shows cocaine use falling year by year, superseded by heroin, opioid painkillers, and weed. But in neighborhoods like the Triangle, where crack never went away, those statistics mean little.

In such places, addicts are still very much in thrall to the rocks, still locked into cycles of addiction, violence, and poverty. And crack's consequences are as crippling as ever. In neighborhoods where crack-dealing street gangs flourish, experts have found increased rates of mental health disorders, sexual assault, suicide, and unemployment, as well as poorer-than-average academic performance.

"The drugs are here, the poverty is here, and everything that goes with those things—domestic violence, substance abuse, crime—are here too," says Toni LaFleur, a single mother and beautician who lives on MLK just outside the Triangle. Her son Devon, she says, recently started selling weed part-time for the Bloods. "If you need proof of how bad things are here, just look at the schools."

Indeed, the graduation rate at Hempstead High School, located two blocks from the heart of the Triangle, is 38 percent—the lowest among Long Island's 124 public school districts. Gang fights on the street regularly carry over onto school property. And the institution serves as a fertile recruitment zone for future Crips and Bloods, as well as other area crews.

"Biggest mistake I ever made was moving to this neighborhood," LaFleur says. "Before, when we lived in Brooklyn, there weren't any Crips or Bloods on our street. But we got priced out. Now, on top of everything else, I've got to worry about my son selling drugs out there, where he could get shot anytime. It's no way to live. It's hell, is what it is."

CHAPTER SIX

Revenge

Just when you think you've seen it all, little Bolo come out blasting like John mothafucking Wayne.

—Ice

A black Denali pulls up at a Crips drug corner on Linden Place, Nas's "N.Y. State of Mind" pounding from its speakers. Tyrek, in the passenger seat, stares down each member of his corner crew while chewing on a toothpick. Tony, in the driver's seat, steps out to survey the operation: Savant Sharpe, wearing a Darryl Strawberry Mets jersey, is handling lookout duties today; "Bolo" Jay Woodson, who's in the midst of a tryout for the crew, acts as tout; Dice Beckles and Skinny Pete, decked out in blue Crips bandanas, serve as corner muscle.

"Look alive, niggas—ain't even lunchtime yet," Tony says, his voice strong and resonant. "This wartime, so you all got to be on y'alls toes. Morning, noon, and night, them guns going to be busting. Any Bloods fuck with you, anybody drive by looking like they about to do some shit, anybody mouth off, you handle it like soldiers. No exceptions. Nobody get a pass for nothing. Far as the Shop goes, you don't let no niggas cop if they ain't got the full amount. No mothafucking IOUs, aight?"

The young men all nod in unison.

"This the way we bang on a mothafucking daily basis," Tony says. "Every time we see them Bloods up in here, we popping at them, we clapping at them. Shit's about to get real after what they did to Crazy Ray. Aight?"

The hustlers nod again, seeming excited by the prospect of exacting vengeance.

"One other piece of business, then I'll let y'all get back to work. Name of the product changing as of right now. We calling the two-for-one bags 'Ghost Rider,' because when you smoke that shit, you feel all Johnny Blaze."

The Hempstead gangs change the names of their product every few weeks, even though there's generally no difference between one "brand" and another. Before Ghost Rider, Crips' vials and baggies had been called "Luda," which had replaced "Scarface," and before that, "Reebok." Just like the advertising executives on Madison Avenue, gangs know that finding the perfect name for their brand can make it more desirable to customers, even if nothing about the product itself changes. Crips touts must either hype the brand with success or face Tony's wrath. And selling the two-for-one bags is a priority, since they get customers hooked on a higher dose of crack. When the "special" is over and prices double, most pipeheads will fork over the extra cash without a second thought.

A few blocks away on MLK, Tony tells his men, Bloods are slinging their own newly named product: "Occupy."

"You tell our customers that Occupy package is weak, and they need to get turned on to Ghost Rider for twice as much at the same price," Tony says. "This shit going to sell itself because it's premium, but you all being vocal ain't going to hurt none."

Tony looks around at each of the gangsters, eyebrows raised, expecting questions. Bolo Jay's hand shoots up.

"Yeah?" Tony says.

"Yo, why we calling it Ghost Rider?" asks Bolo.

"Because that's what the fuck we calling it, nigga," Tony says.

"But why him instead of a better comic book character?" Bolo continues. "Why don't we call it Spider-Man or Hulk? Yo, even better, what about Beast from X-Men? Beast off the chain."

The Crips standing in the street all laugh, except for Tony.

"Yo, you think this funny?" Tony says.

Bolo is still a Crips associate, not yet an official member. And in Tony's view, he's been acting like a little kid for weeks now instead of stepping up during his tryout shifts and proving he belongs. There are also suspicions among some Crips—though no hard proof—that Bolo's been skimming coke from the gang's packages to sell on the side. Even worse, there's talk that he'd fed cops information about Big Mac's murder. Bolo, undeterred by those previous strikes against him, keeps on talking.

"Nah, I'm just saying, if the name going to be a superhero, it should be the best superhero, right?"

Tony doesn't answer. Instead, he pulls a rubber-gripped Glock from his waistband and slams it into Bolo's nose, splitting it open in a spray of blood and mucus. The rest of the crew watches in silence, backing away from their bleeding compatriot. No one dares go over to help him—not until Tony climbs back in the Denali and drives off. Tyrek beside him continues to suck on his toothpick, smiling at the bloody scene left in his wake.

Such acts of sadistic violence, so seemingly out of proportion to the incidents that trigger them, are daily occurrences in the Triangle. Perhaps, Tony confides later, he's guilty of posturing, of trying to appear tougher than he needed to in front of the younger Crips and, in doing so, behaved more cruelly than the circumstance required. On the other hand, maybe it was a perfectly reasonable response, he says, given that the memory of Crazy Ray's murder, and Tony's overwhelming desire to avenge it, is still fresh.

"When we going to hit back for Ray?" Tony asks his boss as they cruise through Crips territory, surveying their other corners.

"We just waiting for the right moment," Tyrek says.

On a rainy night in March, the right moment comes.

A deafening spray of semiautomatic gunfire echoes down MLK just after sunset, causing all the queued-up pipeheads and children playing in project yards to hit the deck. The Bloods stationed outside the Park Lake

Apartments draw their weapons, aiming at the darkened street. They squeeze their triggers fast as they can, guns going off everywhere now. MLK is quickly shrouded in clouds of gun smoke and orange muzzle-flash explosions, the air stinking of gunpowder, sweat, and burned rubber.

The Park Lake apartments, a low-income housing development on Martin Luther King Jr. Drive, served as the Hempstead Bloods' headquarters and primary drug-dealing location.
KEVIN DEUTSCH

Then there is silence; nothing in the street but shadows. No drive-by cars. No Crips.

The sounds of gunshots have a way of echoing through the maze-like project yards along MLK, making it seem as though one's being attacked from all directions. Such grim acoustics make it hard to determine the location from which bullets are flying. The mystery on this night is solved by Doc Reed, who comes bolting around the corner of Oakland Street onto MLK.

"Yo, Lamar shot!" Doc says. "It looks bad, yo. He took one in the chest."

Doc runs back around the corner, leading the rest of his crew to where Lamar, Ice's fast-rising protégé, lay curled up in the street. The chest wound has soaked the front of Lamar's shirt in blood. He's muttering something unintelligible, his body trembling, his eyes rolling up toward the back of his head.

"Nigga having a seizure," says Doc. "Damn."

The crew argues over whether to call 911, weighing the potential for lifesaving medical care versus the risk of police interrogations sure to follow. The dilemma is rendered moot by an MLK resident who'd watched the scene unfold through his bedroom window and called police. As the ear-splitting bleeps of ambulance sirens and squad cars draw closer, several Bloods stand over Lamar, offering words of encouragement.

"Ambos coming—you be aight, Lamar," says Big Boy. "Hold on, yo."

"They going to stitch you back up like nothing happened," Doc says, kneeling so that his face is just above Lamar's. "That slug ain't shit."

But Lamar soon stops trembling, his fluttering eyes going still.

"Dang," Doc says.

People are starting to come out of their apartments, drawn by the approaching sirens and shouts in the street. Rhonda Lovejoy, Lamar's girlfriend, stumbles out onto MLK in her blue bathrobe, looking bleary-eyed, and walks up to the growing crowd gathered around the body. She gets close enough to see it's Lamar and lets out a mournful scream paramedics will later claim to have heard from a full mile away. Her howl seems to rouse the Bloods from the morbid trance they'd fallen into, watching their friend die.

"Yo, let's go before five-o get here," Doc says.

They run to their cars and speed off, leaving Rhonda standing alone over the corpse, her screams drowning out the shouted orders of policemen as the cavalry arrives. Cops fan out across MLK and the Triangle, rounding up junkies and gangbangers for questioning. Detectives door-knock apartments and homes, announcing they'll be enforcing old warrants for everyone in the area unless witnesses start cooperating. But the threat does little to sway residents on either side of the war zone; they all know a night or two in county lockup is preferable to the fates that await them should they talk to cops about a gang murder.

The Bloods who'd left Lamar to bleed out head for East New York, Brooklyn, where an affiliate set maintains a safe house. There, they meet up with Steed and Ice to figure out the crew's next move. Meanwhile, several Crips involved in Lamar's shooting rush to their own safe houses in the nearby neighborhoods of Wyandanch and Central Islip. When detectives show up at the Crips Triangle clubhouse, the place is quiet, not a single hustler slinging outside.

"We ain't done shit," Flex announces as Delahunt pounds on the door. "If you ain't got no warrant, you ain't coming in."

At nearly every address in the neighborhood, residents claim to have been asleep when the shooting happened. No residents admit to hearing or seeing anything that might help detectives. In fact, for all the anguish exhibited by Rhonda Lovejoy and other local noncombatants over Lamar's murder, no one—not even Lamar's own aunt, Donna Crawford—will cooperate with police.

"I don't know anything," she tells detectives the night of his shooting, even though she has an excellent idea of who shot her nephew, and why. Gossip about fresh murders travels fast in the Triangle—just not to cops—ricocheting around the contained space much like the sounds of gunfire.

"Yes, you do," Delahunt replies.

"You a mind reader?"

"Yeah, sort of."

Crawford can't help but smile. She respects the detectives and appreciates the fact they have a job to do. But they know as well as she does what could happen if she talks to them about Lamar's killing.

"We can protect you," the other detective says, declaring the Crips "won't get near you."

But when she asks what guarantees can be made for her safety, they promise neither round-the-clock protection nor relocation.

"We're not the FBI, ma'am," says Delahunt.

What they do promise is a police cruiser stationed outside her house at all times for the foreseeable future, rapid response to any 911 calls made from her home, and occasional police escorts for her and her family.

"Not good enough," she says.

Crawford refuses to lose another child to the streets, she tells them, and if that means her nephew's killer remains free, she'll swallow that bitter pill.

"About fifteen years ago, my son was killed in a shooting, and I helped the police find the boy who did it," she explains. "The day after that boy got arrested, his gang came back and killed my other son in retaliation for my giving the cops information."

That second son died in her arms, she says, and the image of him breathing his last breath enters her dreams most every night.

"I only have one son left," she says, "and I'd rather all the criminals in the world walk free than put him at risk by talking to you all."

"I'm sorry for your loss, ma'am," says Delahunt.

"Don't be sorry," Crawford says. "Just understand my reality."

Impoverished residents like Donna have little chance of ever escaping the Triangle, since housing costs in nearly every other neighborhood—both in Long Island and New York City—are more than they can afford. Being trapped here necessitates they maintain a cold-eyed realism about their circumstances. Seeking justice from police for past grievances, even the murder of loved ones, will not bring the departed back. And, more than likely, it will land the justice-seekers in a grave of their own. So they hold their tongues, hoping for a day when the gangs are gone and things are different.

———

Lamar's funeral a few days later is a sea of red, with Bloods from across Long Island and New York City in attendance. Absent among the mourners are the parents of the deceased. Lamar's father, once a beloved car mechanic and handyman in the neighborhood, succumbed to a heroin overdose about five years earlier. Less than a year later, his mother began chasing crack to dull some of her grief. As her addiction worsened, Lamar and his little brother and sister spent more and more time alone, forced to take care of each other. One day, their mom disappeared with her dealer-turned-boyfriend and never came back, leaving Lamar, a child himself, to raise his two younger siblings.

"He deserved better than he got," Donna Crawford says during the eulogy. "But justice will be served. Maybe not from the police, but from the Lord on high."

At a Bloods safe house after the burial, Ice tells Steed he wants to know with certainty which Crip shot Lamar. There are rumors, Steed says, that Bolo Jay did the shooting, with Rock behind the wheel. But Ice struggles to wrap his mind around that dynamic. In targeting his protégé Lamar, Ice says, Tyrek must have known the Bloods' response would be swift and overwhelming, regardless of whether the mission succeeded. Why, then, would Tyrek have tasked one of his newest, least-experienced foot soldiers, Bolo Jay, with the drive-by? And could Bolo really have carried out such a meticulously planned hit, one in which Lamar had been caught alone and off guard in the open, with no gun on him? To Ice, the hit seemed more like Rock's handiwork, and the rumor about his being the wheelman suggested he'd indeed played a significant role.

"I'm seeing Rock's fingerprints all over this," Ice tells Steed. "Even if Bolo did pull the trigger, it *had* to be Rock doing the recon, planning that shit, telling Bolo exactly what to do, how to do it, when to do it."

"So you want them both done?" Steed asks. "Rock *and* Bolo?"

"I want them both, no question," Ice says with practiced nonchalance, ordering the killings the way he might a drink. "Sooner the better. Let them shells off."

⚊⚊

Bolo, hiding out a few miles away, knows he's a marked man.

He's holed up in a Crips stash apartment in Uniondale, prohibited from leaving for any reason. Rock has even dispatched two soldiers there to make sure he doesn't try to run off or communicate with anyone until the heat dies down. The Big Homies don't want the kid doing anything stupid in the aftermath of his triumph.

"Yo, when I'm going to be able to get up outta here?" Bolo asks his minders.

"When we say so, nigga."

They watch the Knicks game, Bolo crammed between the two much larger men on the living room couch. They have some Chinese food delivered, and when the game ends, one of the Bloods soldiers flips through the channels until he lands on *Jurassic Park*. Bolo can't take his eyes off the TV.

"Whoa," he says when the T-Rex makes its first appearance on-screen. "What's that?"

"Nigga, you ain't never seen no dinosaur before?" one of the soldiers asks.

"Nah," Bolo says with awe in his voice, his mouth slightly agape. In the television's glow, he looks younger than his sixteen years. And for a moment, both soldiers grin with what seems to be real amusement, remembering, perhaps, being awed by such things when they were children.

"These things were real?" Bolo asks a little later. "Like, walking around, for real? Before there were humans?"

"Yeah, son," one of the men says. "Ain't you learned about them in school?"

Bolo shakes his head and munches on an egg roll. He hasn't been to school in a year, not since his mom fatally overdosed on heroin, leaving him to care for his eight-year-old brother, Alex. Between taking care of him, dealing with their crack-addicted foster mother, and working shifts on Tyrek's corners, there's no time for academics, he explains.

"I didn't like going to school nohow," he says. "Them classes were hard."

Instead of doing homework, Bolo's done his best to be a good soldier, showing up to his tryout shifts on time every day, trying to make sure his corner profit tallies are correct. But math has always been his weakness. Sometimes, he can't calculate a pipehead's proper change; no matter how hard he racks his brain, he ends up making a mistake. A few boys in the gang think he's stealing, he knows. But Bolo loves running with the Crips more than anything, he says, and would never take from his own crew.

"I wanted to be Crip my whole life."

Tony's pistol-whipping him in the Triangle three weeks earlier had been humiliating, he says, but not as bad as when Delahunt stopped him in a bodega and started asking about Big Mac's killing. Bolo didn't tell him anything, other than to say he hadn't the slightest idea who did it. Delahunt kept pressing anyway, moving in front of Bolo whenever he tried to leave. To anyone passing by, it must have looked like they were having a real conversation, Bolo knew. On his way home from the store, he prayed word of the encounter wouldn't get back to the Big Homies. But it quickly did, spurring rumors he'd turned snitch.

The humiliation from the pistol-whipping hadn't waned, nor had Bolo's desire to prove he wasn't a rat. So when Tony had asked him if he'd help kill Lamar, Bolo saw it as a chance to get back the respect he'd lost. He believed such an act would redeem him, while proving once and for all that he was loyal to the Crips.

The following day, Rock had driven him to a shooting range in Suffolk County for target practice. Bolo had fired several guns, but told Rock he felt most comfortable handling the Glock 9mm. Rock secured a clean one for him and explained he'd be doing the driving while Bolo did the shooting. This was a test of his loyalty as much as anything, Bolo knew.

"If you miss that nigga or he don't go down from what you hit him with, I'll finish him off," Rock said. "Just aim true, young'un."

Bolo did, squeezing off six rounds and hitting Lamar with three, including a chest shot that had pierced his left lung.

"Nice shooting," Rock had said as they sped away from the scene. "You a natural."

Bolo had been giddy on the ride to the stash apartment afterward, feeling for the first time that he'd earned his place in the crew. He'd envisioned getting a hero's welcome, endless daps and shout-outs from his fellow soldiers for dropping his first body, maybe even a celebratory blunt packed with bomb weed. But when Rock dropped him off, there was no one around except these two hard-looking soldiers.

This treatment makes perfect sense to Tyrek, who fancies himself a kind of gangland military strategist.

"Keep the young'un hungry," he says of Bolo, and "he'll be motivated when it's time to hit again." Deny him praise, keep him away from his exultant fellow gangsters, and he'll become the focused, clear-eyed killer Rock needs by his side at a time like this, Tyrek says. The kid's a blank canvas, and the Crips can paint him any way they'd like.

"I'm in a chess game with those slobs," Tyrek says of the Bloods. "Bolo's a part of that game. All of us part of it."

Later, at Seduccion, Ice lights up a blunt, waving off a stripper who's bent over with her backside inches from his face. She offers a lap dance, but Ice tells her he must first talk business with his lieutenants, Steed and Doc.

"You can't find Bolo and Rock?" Ice asks.

"Nah," says Steed. "They hiding out somewhere."

"We still sure they did it?"

"Yeah, it's like we thought. Rock was driving, Bolo shooting."

Ice nods slowly, taking a long pull from his blunt.

"That little bitch manned up," he says, shaking his head, still amazed that Bolo had pulled it off. "Just when you think you've seen it all, little Bolo come out blasting like John mothafucking Wayne."

"His punk ass still ain't got no heart," Steed says. "Probably just closed his eyes and squeezed is all, got lucky and shit."

But there's no denying the significance of the blow Bolo has landed. Before his drive-by, the war appeared to be shifting in the Bloods' favor, due to the murder of Crazy Ray. Now, Ice's crew is seemingly on the ropes, with the Triangle and MLK abuzz over Lamar's death.

"Bottom line is, we looking like bitches right now," Steed says. "Word on the street is we got shook and ran off, retreated and shit."

"Word?" Ice says. "They talking that shit on the block?"

"Shit, they talking like this war be over," Doc says. "That's what everybody be saying.'"

Ice finishes his Hennessy in one gulp, ashes out the blunt, and throws a $20 bill at the dancer spread-eagled on the edge of the stage.

"Let's go then," he says. "This shit can't wait."

They stop at the apartment of one of Ice's girlfriends on Peninsula Boulevard, where the Bloods keep some guns and coke stashed. Inside, he pulls a trunk packed with firearms and ammo out of a bedroom closet. It contains all the crew's favorites: Glock-9s, .22 Berettas, .45 Smith & Wesson pistols and revolvers, a few Saturday Night Specials, two TEC-9s, two sawed-off Remington shotguns, and an AR-15 assault rifle, with what looks to be enough ammo to take down King Kong.

"That's the Crip killa," Ice says, picking up the AR.

Steed grabs two Glocks and a sawed-off, while Doc spins the chamber on a Smith & Wesson revolver, sticks it in his waistband, and pockets a Beretta for good measure. They have enough firepower to mow down anyone they find standing on a Crips corner, Ice says, which is exactly what they plan to do.

"Time to ride," says Steed.

⸺ ⸻

They roam the streets in search of a car to use for the mission, ideally something subtle and nondescript, a model no one will remember. They settle on an off-white Dodge Stratus with heavy tints. Ice expertly hot-wires it and then they drive until they're just around the corner from the Crips' Triangle clubhouse. Dice Beckles, who's on lookout duty tonight, doesn't seem to notice the Stratus's arrival. The Shop is up and running but traffic is light, with just a few drive-up customers pressing $10 and $20 bills into the tout's hands and hardly any foot traffic. It's been raining on and off since morning, keeping most of the pipeheads indoors while waiting for the clouds to move out.

Doc checks the AccuWeather app on his iPhone every few minutes, knowing the rain and fog are supposed to get worse as the evening wears on. He keeps Ice and Steed abreast of the forecast, since the men have laid out a plan that aims to take advantage of the foul weather. They'll wait until the Crips' midnight shift change, when Tony, Flex, and sometimes Tyrek himself show up to supervise the Saturday-night rush. Then, they'll open fire. Their goal is to "decapitate" the Crips leadership, Ice says, to "cut off the head of that ugly-ass snake."

They hold guns in their laps and stash others under the Stratus's seats, waiting for the Big Homies to show. Shooting in the rain won't be ideal, they know. But their plan calls for such an overwhelming use of firepower, it's hard to imagine them missing their trio of targets. With fog and downpours keeping visibility low in the Triangle, the Crips will be hard-pressed to even see where the bullets are coming from, much less return fire with any degree of accuracy.

"Be like shooting fish in a barrel, yo," Ice says. The men watch the digital clock on the dashboard. Another hour until midnight. "I can't wait to see these bitch niggas run when we start popping off."

What the Bloods leaders don't know is that the Crips have decided to change their routine, part of their efforts to make a retaliatory strike more difficult. The directive came down from Tyrek two nights earlier: No Big Homies on the street until further notice. Lower-level dealers, working longer shifts to make up for the loss of manpower, would run all Crips corners.

Knowing his dealers, runners, touts, and lookouts would likely protest the longer shifts, Tyrek's making it worth their while, nearly doubling their wages. The crew can afford it now, their coffers swollen thanks to a newly opened corner in Uniondale and some bulk sales they'd made to independent dealers in Staten Island and Queens.

Midnight comes and goes without the Crips leaders showing, but Doc, Steed, and Ice sit tight, believing Tyrek and his lieutenants will arrive at any moment. Another hour passes, then two. Despite the bad weather, the late-night party crowd turns out in droves for the Ghost Rider vials. Many of them return an hour or two later to buy more.

Still, no Big Homies show their faces.

"Something up, man," Steed says. "Flex and Tony here like clockwork every Saturday. And Tyrek almost always check in, too. They must've changed shit up."

At five a.m., the Crips dealing crew closes down the Shop, getting into their cars to drive home or walking back to their Triangle apartments. On the busiest sales night of the week, none of their bosses had shown. The Bloods head home, too, vowing to finish the job as soon as they get a fix on their targets' whereabouts.

"These niggas was ready for us," Ice says. "That's aight, though. They can't hide forever."

But the Crips' Big Homies are disciplined and careful. They stick to their plan and are rarely seen in public over the next few weeks. Despite the Bloods having enlisted an army of neighborhood informants—mostly pipeheads paid in vials—Tyrek, Tony, and Flex's whereabouts remain a mystery as April arrives in Hempstead.

Thwarted by the Crips, Ice begins planning a different move aimed at reasserting the Bloods' position in the neighborhood.

"We going to hit 'em where it hurts," Ice says. "We going after one of their women."

CHAPTER SEVEN

Extreme Tactics

What that man said they did to her just ain't right.

—Darren

Leticia "Black Widow" Lewis is walking home after a long runner shift, her eyes cast downward, her mind on weekend plans. She doesn't notice the Ford SUV following her, even when it speeds up and pulls alongside her as she turns onto Laurel Avenue. She doesn't look up, even when a masked Bloods soldier steps out of the Ford and, quietly as he can, moves toward her. Leticia is one of the few Crips employees who doesn't carry a gun these days, believing she won't be targeted because she's a woman. But such rules don't apply in a gang war this intense. In such a climate, the Hempstead Bloods have decided that if Tyrek, Tony, and Flex want to "hide out like bitches" after what they did to Lamar, then it's only fair the females they run with pay the price.

Leticia doesn't hear her abductor's footsteps until he's just behind her, and by then it's too late. He spins her around and clobbers her face with a pistol, grabs her by her hair, and throws her over his shoulder. People in their homes must surely hear her crying out. Around here, though, screams are too common to cause real alarm. Like gunfire and police sirens, they're a kind of white noise in the Triangle, the sounds people in any war zone learn to ignore after a while.

Leticia is tossed into the SUV's backseat as it speeds off. Inside, her captors blindfold and hog-tie her, punching and burning her with lit cigarettes. By the time the SUV arrives at its destination, she's bleeding from her nose and mouth, her skin covered in circular burn marks.

They carry her inside a building and up to a room barren but for a soiled mattress on the floor. There, they undress her at gunpoint. For the next twenty-four hours, she's raped repeatedly, sometimes by groups of men, sometimes by one at a time. She resists at first, screaming, biting, and squirming in an effort to break free of the plastic zip ties binding her arms and feet. But the men beat her for resisting and she's soon too exhausted, in too much pain, to keep fighting.

The first men to rape her are those whose voices she'd heard in the car. Then more arrive and take their turns. Still blindfolded, she's allowed small meals—cold-cut sandwiches and Coca-Cola—every few hours. Her captors force her to swallow uppers so that she doesn't fall asleep. One rapist, who's particularly rough with her, grabs her hand and sucks on her fingers as he penetrates her. She feels a scar running across his chin and makes a mental note of it, hoping it will help her identify him later.

When there are no more men left to serve, when Leticia's face is so bruised and covered in dried blood that she's no longer recognizable, they let her go. She's driven to the same corner she'd been kidnapped from twenty-four hours earlier. There, she is tossed, half-naked and blindfolded, onto the cold pavement. Her abductors speed away. It begins to rain as she lies there, trembling in the road. And it's a long time before she can gather the energy to stand up and walk home.

At first, Leticia doesn't speak of the attack to anyone. She calls Tyrek and says she needs a few weeks off to attend to some family business. But she's really holed up in her apartment day after day, nursing her injuries and trying to get her mind right. She knows that if the Crips find out what happened, they'll hunt down and probably kill the men who did this to her—men she assumes are Bloods and their associates. But she also knows the stigma she'll carry should her crew learn of the attack. She'll be known in the neighborhood as the girl who got "gangbanged" by the Bloods. She won't be able to walk anywhere without wondering if the men staring at her on the street were among those who raped her. And the Crips would eventually cast her out of their circle, she believes, unable to look at her without being reminded of the defeat she represented.

Leticia's secret is kept until a month or so later, when one of her rapists brags about the attack to an acquaintance of his, a building maintenance man named Darren, who happens to go back a ways with Leticia. Upset by the story he'd heard, Darren asks around for her, wanting to see if she's all right. He knows she runs with the Crips, so he drops by their clubhouse in the Triangle to ask about her whereabouts. The Big Homies aren't around when Darren shows, so a Crips foot soldier calls Tyrek to tell him there's a man looking for Leticia.

"I'll be right there," Tyrek says. "Tell him not to go nowhere."

Tyrek suspected from the start that something was wrong with Leticia, whom he hasn't seen on the street in weeks. He has called her several times since she asked for time off, and though she insisted everything was fine, Tyrek sensed she was hiding something. Thinking Darren may know what's behind her withdrawal, Tyrek has Rock pick him up and drive him to the clubhouse. There, Darren tells them the story he'd heard from his Bloods acquaintance.

"What that man said they did to her," Darren says, "just ain't right."

Tyrek thanks him, slips him $100 for his troubles, and sends him on his way with instructions to keep relaying any intelligence of interest to the Crips.

"Drive me down to Leticia's crib," Tyrek tells Rock.

At Leticia's house, the men bang on the door for fifteen minutes before she finally gets out of bed and opens up. She is rail-thin and pale, so different from the girl they remember running their packages.

"You need to talk to me, Tish," Tyrek says. "Tell me what happened."

She's hesitant at first, but once she sees the men have no intention of leaving, Leticia relents. Through tears, she tells them all the details, relating what the attackers said to her, what they fed her, what the place smelled like. She tells them about the man with the scar on his chin, the way it made her sick when she touched it.

"Steed, that mothafucka," Tyrek says.

She chain-smokes Marlboro Lights as she tells her story, crying hysterically at times but always gathering herself and continuing. By the time she finishes, Tyrek and Rock have worked themselves into states of rage unprecedented even for them. Soon they're out the door and in Rock's car, speeding toward MLK. They park near the projects, boost an unlocked Camry, and roll through Bloods territory in search of Steed.

"Nigga's going to wish he stayed in LA," Tyrek says.

CHAPTER EIGHT

Eye for an Eye

Revenge is always, always *on my mind.*

—LETICIA

Before committing a murder, Rock always says a prayer. Clutching his gold crucifix charm, he'll ask God to forgive him for what he's about to do; he'll ask for mercy and understanding, so that he'll be granted entrance to heaven one day. With Steed in his crosshairs, he adds a caveat: "If I got to burn in hell for doing this nigga, it's worth it," Rock says, squeezing the trigger of his MAC-10.

Muzzle flashes light up the car's interior as the smell of gunpowder carries through the stale June air. From her couch, Hempstead resident Nadine Johnson sees the flashes, hears the gun blasts, followed by tires screeching. She dials 911, looks out her window, and sees the bodies of two young men splayed in the street.

"Better come fast," she tells the operator. "People shot."

The Bloods on the ground are Steed and one of the set's lookouts, Spider Rick. Steed, shot in his leg, limps away from the scene before authorities arrive. Rick, his wound more severe, is rushed to the hospital by paramedics. Both men leave behind small pieces of flesh—remains torn off by bullets and left to bake in the next day's intense afternoon sun.

When the detectives arrive, Nadine Johnson tells them that she didn't get a look at the getaway car she heard peel out. Nor did she see the men inside it.

"All I know is it happened very fast," she says. "And the smell . . . it smelled like flesh burning out there. The bullets went in, the smell came out. The worst scent I've ever smelled."

Detectives check security footage from local businesses facing the street, but none show the getaway car. They fan out to interview Bloods and Crips, believing the shooting is linked to their gang war. But no one gives them anything tangible to go on.

"Snitches get stitches? Fuck that," Delahunt says. "What about the stitches it's going to take to sew that kid back together? Why doesn't that part of it matter to them?"

The shell casings littering the scene are their best evidence, but they need the gun that fired them if they're going to find the shooter. No easy task, they know. In the Triangle, recovering a hot weapon can be an excruciating process that takes weeks, months, or even years, if it happens at all. In 2010, just two illegal guns were recovered in Hempstead, according to state records. The following year, police found none.

"Sometimes it feels like a fucking lost cause," says Delahunt. "Like it's a zoo, and we're the zoo minders."

The next morning, Tyrek sees a report about the shooting on the news. One man, Spider Rick, wounded, but expected to survive. No mention of a second victim—the intended target, Steed—even though Tyrek saw him take at least one slug.

"Nigga's got nine lives," Tyrek says.

"No worries, yo," says Rock. "I got this."

He calls up two of his soldiers in Brooklyn and orders them to find Ice's sister, mother, niece, or any other close female relative.

"Do what you need to do to make this even," Rock says. "Eye for an eye and shit."

By week's end, they've found an address for Ice's sister in Yonkers, where she lives with her husband and his son from a prior marriage. Francine Williams is a thirty-three-year-old retail clothing store worker who hasn't spoken with her brother in years, wanting nothing to do with him or his gang. She'd been a heroin addict in her younger days, supplied by her own brother's criminal associates. But she'd cleaned up her act years ago and put as much distance between her old life, and Ice, as she could.

She's long anticipated a knock on the door or phone call from authorities, notifying her of her brother's death, so when the doorbell rings just after eleven p.m. on a sweltering Saturday night in early July, she's expecting men in uniform. She's alone; her husband and his son are upstate for a long-awaited weekend at the Baseball Hall of Fame in Cooperstown.

When she opens the door, the men standing before her aren't in uniform. And from the flashy jewelry on their necks and wrists, she knows right away they're not cops. She gets a sinking feeling in her stomach.

"I'm sorry, can I help you?" she says.

"Yeah, you can, sweetie," one of them says, stepping past her before she can shut the door. She's just begun to scream when the other Crips soldier covers her mouth and forces her at gunpoint into the bedroom.

"You can thank your brother for this," he says.

The sexual assault is quick and brutal, leaving Francine sobbing and badly bruised. Afterward, when her attackers are gone, she rifles through a drawer full of old papers and finds her brother's cell-phone number, the one she'd held on to in case of an emergency. She dials and waits, imagining what she'll say, framing the words she'll use to blame him for the evil he has brought into her life. The line rings and rings, but there's no answer. Not even voicemail. Ice was always careful that way, she knows, using burner phones for almost all his calls.

When her husband and his son return two days later, Francine acts as if nothing's amiss. She's too ashamed to speak of what her brother's rivals did to her.

One day after work, she drives to downtown Yonkers and buys a bag of heroin. She returns to the corner the next day, and the day after that. One of the bags of heroin she buys is cut with an extremely high dose of fentanyl, a painkiller roughly a hundred times stronger than morphine. Within minutes of injecting it, Francine stops breathing. A passerby finds her slumped over in her car two hours later, cold to the touch.

The rapes of Leticia and Francine are not anomalies. Crips and Bloods members in eleven sets across Long Island and New York City say their crews have perpetrated sex crimes in an effort to lower enemy morale, deter retaliatory shootings, encourage payment of drug debts, or meet other gang objectives, especially during prolonged turf conflicts. The gangsters see sexual violence as a strategic and tactical weapon, as important to their arsenal as guns and blades. Some acknowledge personally participating in acts of rape, forced prostitution, and insertion of objects into women's body cavities as instruments of sexual torture.

Such attacks are considered crimes against humanity under international law, but on America's streets, similar crimes perpetrated by gang members are rarely reported or punished, according to victims, perpetrators, and police.

Like Leticia and Francine, many victims don't report rapes to law enforcement because they fear retaliation from their attackers. As a result, culprits are rarely held to account. When victims do report gang-related sexual assaults to friends or family, payback is usually doled out by male relatives, or whichever gang the victim is connected to. It's street justice, since the nonviolent variety is often not enough to quell a victim's desire for revenge.

Crips and Bloods say women and young girls are routinely raped because their boyfriends or male relatives owe the gang money for drugs or guns. Other victims are targeted because their boyfriends are rival gang members suspected of carrying out drive-bys. In some cases, rape victims are selected at random—a tactic aimed at terrifying the population within an opposing gang's territory, and keeping them from snitching about gang activities. Random sexual assaults are also used by rival gangs to pressure civilians to withdraw support for their neighborhood's gang, leaving that gang more vulnerable to police raids and surprise attacks from enemy crews.

"It's the deepest kind of revenge you can get, besides straight murder," says Flex Butler, the Crips lieutenant. "You do that to somebody's sister, somebody's girl, some bitch who runs with them, and they get all torn up over that. It's the ultimate disrespect to your enemy . . . doing their women like that."

During his gang career, Flex says he's participated in at least three group sexual assaults against women affiliated with the Bloods. One of the girls was just fifteen, the younger sister of a former Hempstead Blood, Leroy "Brick" Brewer, who'd stolen $2,000 worth of cocaine from a Crips stash house.

"Brick was hiding from us," Flex says. "So we got his sister when she was walking home from school. She fought hard, but there was a lot of us."

On the Bloods side of Hempstead, the preferred mode of sexual assault is also gang rape. Members say they learned the tactic from a Queens-based Bloods crew they're close with—a set that habitually uses rape to run competing dealers off their corners.

"The way they do it in Queens is, if a boy don't want to leave a corner after they told him a couple of times that he need to, they find his house, where his people stay at, and they go after his sister or his niece or his moms," says Steed. "Just whoever they can grab while they there."

His own set has found such attacks build camaraderie among newer and older members, Steed says, giving them a shared, twisted experience to bond over.

"It sound crazy, but that shit do bring you together sometimes, especially if it's good and she ain't trying to hit and fight everybody."

Doc Reed says he generally chooses to watch such attacks rather than partake. "I don't want to get no HIV or STDs," he says. "I don't know where any of these hos have been. I ain't taking the chance."

For victims of sexual assaults perpetrated by Crips and Bloods, the impact—both physical and emotional—is immeasurable. Leticia says she has had a series of medical problems as a result of her attack, including genital herpes and gynecologic fistula. She undergoes weekly psychological counseling and believes certain traumatic memories of her assault will never leave her.

"I wish I could forget about it," Leticia says. "But it's something that's always with me—when I wake up, when I go to work, when I go to sleep, when I'm walking around or on the bus. Wherever I go, it's there."

For months, she tried to erase those painful memories with alcohol and drugs, she says.

"But there wasn't enough liquor or coke in the world to cover up that pain. I realized I would just have to deal with it head-on, get treatment, work through what I was feeling. But what I feel most strongly, still and probably always will, is hate. I hate those boys for what they did. They're animals, and I will never, ever forgive them, even if they came begging, I wouldn't. Revenge is always, *always* on my mind."

Francine, Ice's sister, also turned to drugs to deal with the emotional trauma from her rape—something her husband discovered by reading her journals after she died. She'd never once mentioned the attack to him, he said, nor hinted that anything went awry while he'd been in Cooperstown.

"She kept everything locked up inside of her, all that pain and anger," he says. "It was what they did to her that killed her. The drugs were just a vehicle, just the end of the process that started once they violated her."

Some victims of sexual violence perpetrated by Crips and Bloods find solace in spending time together, sharing stories of their experiences in an effort to heal and move on with their lives. In East New York, Brooklyn, a territorial war between Crips and Bloods sets in 2009 and 2010 became so dangerous for women associated with the gangs that some of them moved out of the neighborhood and into a home in southern Queens. There, they live together to this day, cooking for one another and participating in group therapy.

One of the victims, Tania, says Bloods members raped her because her second cousin—a Crip whose immediate family lived with her own in a large apartment—participated in a drive-by that wounded two set leaders. In an alley behind a liquor store, she says, several gangsters bound, beat, urinated on, and raped her numerous times. They stopped the assault only when a Good Samaritan walking his dog stumbled upon the scene and scared them off.

"What they did to me . . . should never happen to anybody. The worst part of it was seeing them around the neighborhood after that. And they said, 'You tell anybody, we'll kill you.' So I didn't say anything for a few months, until I was sure I could get out of there and they couldn't find me."

When she finally confided to a female friend about the attack, the woman put her in touch with another victim assaulted during the same gang war. That victim, a social worker named Linette, had recently opened the Queens safe house, where she already lived with five other women raped during the conflict. Tania moved in with them a few weeks later.

"My attacker was this 250-pound guy, a Blood they called Tub, because he was big as a bathtub," says Linette. "They sent him after me because I had a boyfriend at the time who owed the Bloods a lot of money for a package [of coke] they'd fronted him. It got stolen, and he didn't have the money to pay them. He asked for time to get the money together, and they said he could have a little more time. But then they found out he went to some Crips he was friends with to ask for money, and they didn't like how he was dealing with the situation, I guess. I guess they saw it as him being tight with their enemy, set on top of already owing them money, and they knew I was with him.

"So Tub followed me home one day and pushed in behind me when I was coming in my front door. And he raped me. At one point, he said 'This what you get for messing with them Crips.' He took out a blade, some kind of pocketknife or switchblade, and started carving something into my back while he was raping me. When he was gone, I looked in the mirror and saw what he'd carved was a B, for Bloods."

CHAPTER NINE

True Believers

And I'll keep praying for these gangsters on the corners, the ones who can still be saved, until they put me in the ground.

—Marsha Ricks

The sinister plots hatched by one gang against the other don't stop. But neither do Reverend Lyons and his prayer marchers. They return to the Triangle every Friday just before midnight, always with the goal of preventing retaliatory attacks. There are whispers the group may themselves be targeted for sticking their noses in the business of warring gangs. In fact, the risks they face seem to multiply by the week. Savant Sharpe, convinced the marchers are police informants, has promised to hunt them down and kill them if he's proven right. Doc, believing Reverend Lyons is more sympathetic to the Crips' plight than his own gang's, says he'll treat the reverend as a combatant should a gun battle break out while he's in Bloods territory.

Still, the marchers are not dissuaded. "There might be another person shot at any time," Lyons says one muggy Friday in August. "But we pray not."

As they march up Linden Place, plumes of marijuana smoke drift from a dozen open windows. Dealers perched on stoops scurry up to cars or pedestrians who stop to buy crack or weed. Glassy-eyed pipeheads stumble nervously through the Triangle, drawn like moths to the glow of dealer's smartphones.

The marchers pray with local Bloods outside the Park Lake apartments, shown here. There are whispers the group may themselves be targeted for sticking their noses in the business of warring gangs. Savant Sharpe, convinced the marchers are police informants, has promised to hunt them down and kill them if he's proven right.
STEVE PFOST

The Crips slinging on the stoops are immaculately dressed, decked out in sagging designer pants, custom-made baseball jerseys, and the newest LeBrons, Air Jordans, and Dwyane Wades. Platinum chains adorn their necks. Thousand-dollar watches circle their wrists. Tony—who's managing the main Crips shop tonight after a few weeks of staying off the street, per Tyrek's orders—wears diamond earrings thick enough to put his newborn son through college. He's the first of the Crips to notice Lyons coming toward their stoops and nods in the reverend's direction.

This time, none of them wear red.

"We listened," Lyons says.

"Appreciate that," says Tony.

"How y'all been since last time?"

"We aight. You know how it is. Holding it down."

"Glad to see everyone's safe tonight," Lyons says. "Now, you all know what brings us out here?"

"Yeah," says Bolo, fresh off his stash-house sequester and now an official Crips soldier. "You trying to bring Jesus up in our crew."

The Crips all laugh, as do the marchers. The older men can remember hanging with the fathers and uncles of some of these boys back in the day, drinking beers and chasing girls with them in Hempstead. Most are dead now, cut down by bullets or blades following senseless arguments over gang colors, money, women, or drugs.

The marchers join hands and pray with several Crips members outside the gang's headquarters in the Triangle.
STEVE PFOST

After a while, all the ancient beefs bleed together in the Triangle, making it hard to remember which slight cost which man his life. All that matters to the marchers now is saving this new generation of hustlers, making sure they escape the fates of their elders.

"In a way, I guess we *do* want to bring Jesus up in here," says one of the marchers, Calvin Bishop. "But mostly, we just want to pray for you all to be safe and healthy, and ask God to look out for you all and your families, so that he brings you and the people you care about blessings and peace."

"Ain't nothing wrong with some blessings," says Flex Butler. "Blessings always good."

"Would you gentlemen let us pray with you for a moment, then, so that we can seek those blessings?" Lyons asks.

The gangsters ponder his request, silently calculating the potential impact of such a prayer. Would it scare off their customers? Would it be interpreted as a sign of weakness by the Bloods? Were these "old-ass" marchers—however harmless they appeared—actually working for the police, as Savant suspects?

"We're not here to interfere," Lyons says, trying his best to close the deal. "We just want to praise God and ask for his blessings to keep everyone safe tonight."

There's a long pause, punctuated by the sound of a woman crying in the distance.

"Yeah," Tony says. "A little help from on high can't hurt no one around here."

"That's the truth, son," says Lyons.

"So let's do it up," Tony says, his gold teeth twinkling in the porch light.

Each marcher takes the hand of the Crip closest to him. The men circle up, bow their heads, and close their eyes. Lyons breathes in deeply, focusing, wanting badly to reach these boys tonight.

"Dear God," he says, his voice loud and rhythmic as it carries through the Triangle. "We come to you tonight seeking your wisdom and protection. We ask that you give these young men quarter from the pain and violence and suffering on this block, and that you bless them with your everlasting goodwill and favor."

Some of the pipeheads turn to see where the churchly pleas are coming from, wandering toward the prayer circle as Lyons continues. "You, Lord, are the truth and the way. We are here tonight to praise you, to serve you by spreading your Word, and ask you to help heal this struggling neighborhood. Lord, we ask that you look after these young men and keep them safe from harm, that you help heal all wounds in the Village of Hempstead."

"Amen!" the marchers shout.

"We ask that you look after these young men and their families," the reverend continues, "that you shield them from the violence and addiction and troubles that have plagued this community, that you guide them through these streets unscathed and strong."

"Amen!"

"We ask you, Lord, to lead these young men through the darkness and into the light, where they will be safe under your watch. We ask that you carry them toward bright futures and happiness and safety—that you ease them through whatever difficulties they may encounter until they reach calmer seas. Amen."

"Amen!"

Their prayer complete, the Crips and marchers exchange handshakes and first bumps. Others embrace. The prayer, it seems, has left them all feeling good.

"Dang, I done thought I was in church for a minute there," Flex says. "Forgot what it's like to be praying. Been a while."

"Well, we'll help you remember," Bishop says. "A little prayer can never hurt in the Triangle."

"Word," Flex says.

"Be safe," says Lyons. "We'll keep praying for y'all."

"Y'all stay safe, too," Tony says. "For real. Ain't no joke out here."

Once the gangsters are out of earshot, Lyons deems the encounter an unqualified success.

"We're starting to reach them," he says. "They're listening. That's a big step."

The reverend calls his gang intervention program Boots on the Ground, a military term he chose because, like the hustlers whose lives he's trying to save, Lyons views his work as a daily battle, a war fought for the souls of young men.

"You don't win wars by fighting from a distance; you win them by getting in close," Lyons says as he leads his marchers toward the next drug corner. "You can pray for change in a place, but there's something about being *present* in that place, and actually being an agent of the change you're praying for, that allows you to make a greater impact. Get in close, and change is possible. At least, that's what we hope."

As the activists march down Linden Avenue, empty crack vials lay scattered every few feet. Baggies once packed with powder cocaine or crack rocks litter the pavement. An emaciated pipehead wearing a tattered Yankees cap walks alongside the marchers, picking up discarded baggies, holding them up toward streetlights in search of leftovers.

"Got-damn," he says each time he finds one empty.

Calvin Bishop walks toward the pipehead, who's so engrossed in his search for leftover crack he doesn't notice the marchers approaching. Bishop is about to greet him when the man looks up with panic in his eyes.

"Get back!" he yells, reaching into his pocket and coming out with a kitchen knife. It's stained with what looks like peanut butter and a smattering of jelly. Still, it's sharp at the point—sharp enough, by the look of it, to do some damage.

"We don't mean any harm," Bishop says, his voice soft and steady as he looks into the pipehead's eyes. A former crack addict himself who got clean after embracing Christianity, Bishop understands the pipehead's fear and paranoia all too well. "We apologize for disturbing you, sir, sincerely. We were just going to ask if you might be willing to pray with us for a moment."

The man purses his lips, eyes Bishop warily, and puts the knife back in his pocket.

"Y'all going to get yourselves killed walking round here like a bunch of got-damned Boy Scouts," he says. "What you think, you in Disneyland or sumpin'?"

The pipehead walks off to continue his lonely quest through the Triangle, scanning the ground in search of that overlooked rock some fiend always leaves behind—a little chunk of salvation to steel him against another night in a war zone.

"Crack," says Bishop, watching him go. "Turns them into zombies. I wish we could save them all from this kind of life, the way I was saved through the power of prayer. But there's just too many."

From her living room window, Marsha Ricks watches the marchers stride past. Her one-story, bungalow-style home sits at the midway point between the Bloods' and Crips' territories, having served as the unofficial demarcation line—"the DMZ," as she calls it—in more peaceful days. In the past three years, five stray bullets have struck her house, she says. Still, she clings to the hope that things will get better.

"If there's one thing I know about these young men in the gangs, it's that they can't shoot straight," says Ricks, eighty-two, who has lived in Hempstead for more than sixty years. "Lord, they might as well be blind the way they aim. But you never know. The violence could stop one of these days. Things could get better."

Because of errant gunfire, Ricks says she long ago stopped watching TV in her living room at night. That room has the most windows.

"I won't even sit in there to do my crossword. If a bullet comes through the window or tears through the wall, I could die right there in my chair. So I watch TV and do my puzzles in the back bedroom. No windows in there. It's much safer."

Ricks says the neighborhood was once peaceful, back before crack steamrolled its way through Hempstead in the 1980s, coinciding with a recession. She remembers ice-cream trucks coming down her block five times a day, Girl Scout troops going door to door, selling cookies.

"When I was raising my son, this was a wonderful place. The yards were green and well-kept, trees lined the street, and there was no filth in the parks. I loved it here, and my husband and child loved it. In the 1970s, even in the early '80s, I would let him play out in the street, ride his bicycle, or go to the park to play basketball. I didn't worry. There were some gangs, but they didn't go around advertising it. They kept to themselves, moved in their own little world, mostly, and we had nice lives out here. It was safe, clean. People looked out for each other.

"One day, I remember, I started to see dealers on the corners late at night, selling crack. At that time, I didn't know what it was. But I learned real fast, because everybody started talking about it. My friends' kids were walking around like zombies from it, or going to jail for selling it. They said crack was an epidemic, and it really was. But the police didn't do much to stop it. In fact, they seemed to allow the dealers to run free here, so as to keep them out of the white neighborhoods and the nicer parts of Hempstead. Now, you can call that a conspiracy theory, but around here, it was just seen as fact. There was no other way to understand how it could be happening."

One day, Ricks's fed-up husband, Miles, went to tell off the dealers who'd turned his once-attractive street into a vial-strewn drug market. They got in the old man's face, pulled out their guns, and scared him so badly he suffered a fatal heart attack right there in the street.

"Crack stole my husband from me, as far as I'm concerned. And in the years after he passed, it went away in other communities, but not here. You can still buy as much of it as your heart desires, right outside my house."

Ricks says her son, a forty-six-year-old medical student in New Jersey who gave up teaching elementary school math to pursue a career in emergency medicine, is constantly urging her to move—to finally leave behind the pain she endures every time she passes the spot where her husband of forty-six years fell dead.

"But every time I think I can say yes to leaving here and going to live out near my son, I think about my memories of this house, and I say, 'Why should I be the one who has to leave? Why don't these killers and drug dealers and dope fiends leave instead of me?' Now, I know that's not likely to happen, but I'm an optimist. Always have been, and I guess I can't change. But I remember the old days, watching kids playing out there, me and my husband sitting on the porch drinking sodas, waving to our friends driving past. I do believe my grandkids might come back and see the neighborhood like that again one day, after I'm gone. That's one of the things I pray for—that God will take the cancer out of our neighborhood. And I'll keep praying for these gangsters on the corners, the ones who can still be saved, until they put me in the ground."

Long before the Bloods and Crips moved in—before the crack explosion, semiautomatic weapons, and joblessness threatened to destroy the neighborhood—Hempstead was a sleepy, idyllic little village with a seemingly bright future. It began as a meeting place for farmers and traders looking to buy goods and exchange information, a hub of commerce for nineteenth-century Long Islanders.

In the following century, a series of ambitious road-construction projects linked New York City to Long Island, allowing thousands of city residents to visit, and later, to move permanently to Hempstead. The village's population increased more than tenfold between 1870 and 1940, from 2,316 to 20,856, according to Sarah Garland's *Gangs in Garden City*. In one of the earliest examples of white flight, newcomers transformed Hempstead into a bustling modern suburb—one of the country's first—lined with cookie-cutter homes and perfectly manicured lawns.

Long Island neighborhoods with quality housing grew rapidly in the late 1940s and '50s, part of a national trend that saw city residents moving to the suburbs in droves following World War II. Hempstead's rapid expansion created demand for more stores and commercial areas, which went up with astonishing speed alongside giant parking lots for customers, come to town for a day of spending.

The village continued to grow throughout the 1960s, thanks to an influx of immigrants, who'd found economic success in the city and wanted a safer, quieter place to raise their families. Hempstead became known as The Hub due to its history as a commercial center, and the opening of its own Long Island Rail Road station. It was also a retail hub with scores of shops, including the popular Abraham & Straus (A & S) department store. People traveled from all over Long Island to shop there, injecting a flood of new tax money into municipal coffers.

While white flight drove much of Long Island's population boom, scores of minorities flocked there as well, moving to Nassau and Suffolk at more than twice the rate of whites during the 1950s, according to Garland's account. Even as the image of Long Island as an ultrasafe, all-white, suburban utopia took root in the American imagination during the '60s, African Americans were relocating there in huge numbers.

"It's a part of Long Island history that isn't often told, but there was truly a great migration of African-American families like mine in the 1950s and '60s," says Ricks. "We came here looking for the same things—safe streets, good schools, peace and quiet—that whites did."

Blacks often encountered an even deeper discrimination in Long Island's suburbs than they'd experienced in cities. With America embroiled in contentious debates over civil rights, and with racism rampant in many communities, discriminatory housing practices remained common through the 1960s and '70s in Hempstead. Banks routinely refused home loans to blacks, and when minority families *did* find financing, they were often steered to predominantly black neighborhoods. Meanwhile, in mixed neighborhoods, whites couldn't get away soon enough. They fled Hempstead for whiter communities in other parts of Nassau, Suffolk, and Queens.

As whites moved on, Hempstead's aging bungalow-style homes and decaying apartment buildings drew black tenants hoping for their own piece of the suburban dream. They quickly became the majority. And by 1990, the village was nearly all black—a stark example of the suburban segregation already under way in suburbs of Chicago, Kansas City, Fort Lauderdale, St. Louis, West Palm Beach, and dozens of other fast-growing metropolitan areas.

It was during this period that Bloods and Crips found a home in Hempstead. Their arrival coincided with the flight of many village retailers, including A & S, who were taking a beating from malls and big-box stores. Some businesses were abandoned, while arsonists torched others in insurance scams. Crime rose, due in part to the newly arrived gangs and the crack, which became the foundation of their economy.

By the mid-1990s, Hempstead was a shell of its former self. Black families who'd moved there in search of the good life ended up living in the same slum-like conditions they'd tried to escape. Still, Ricks and many hardworking families in her neighborhood believe it can still be saved.

"Even the Triangle, I know, can be redeemed," says Ricks.

Bloods members and prayer marchers cross a street in Hempstead during the gang war. A few blocks away, the Crips are gathered in their clubhouse, plotting a drive-by.
STEVE PFOST

Despite all available evidence, folks in the Triangle have always found a way to believe that better times lay ahead, she says. They believed even as more and more homes were abandoned and occupied by pipeheads and dealers. They believed even as pimps and prostitutes became neighborhood staples. They believed even as the Crips and Bloods arrived in force, set up major drug markets, and unleashed a plague of gun violence. And they believed even as the Triangle became exactly what they'd moved there to escape: a place brimming with poverty, drugs, and death, a kind of free-fire zone where a kid had as good a chance of catching a stray bullet as he did in parts of Syria or Afghanistan.

"We do believe in a better day, because good can outlast evil," Ricks says. "That's what some of these gangsters are. Plain old evil."

Young men like Tyrek, Tony, Ice, and Steed represent everything the "true believers," as Ricks calls Hempstead's good citizens, stand against. The gangsters are among tens of thousands of Bloods and Crips living in the poorest swaths of America's cities and suburbs, mostly uneducated, mostly parentless, raising themselves in packs off the proceeds of petty crimes that later escalate to organized trafficking and violent felonies. In a way, their fates were decided long before they put on gang colors.

"Basically, there ain't no direction I could see going in other than joining [a gang]," says Tyrek. "It's like, natural and shit. That's the path you expected to take. That's the path you *need* to take around here, unless you want to be rolling around by yourself and not have no back. It's how you get a family."

Hempstead's true believers have long tried to change the mentality of these young men, but violence and gang activity have increased nonetheless. Gang-related arrests more than tripled between 1995 and 2001 in Nassau alone, according to Garland's account. In the handful of predominantly minority communities stretching across central Nassau—an area known to police as "the corridor"—more than 300 people have been killed by gun violence over the past fourteen years. More than 80 of those were killed in disputes linked to Bloods or Crips sets and their assorted beefs.[1]

Much of the region's gang violence in 2012, even in Long Island and New York City neighborhoods far from Hempstead, can be traced back to the Triangle war. In ways both seen and unseen, this single Bloods–Crips conflict has sent ripples through the region's underworld establishment, heightening tensions among other sets, pressuring them to retaliate for shootings in Hempstead, and forcing them to lend resources to the Triangle war effort.

"The battle over turf in the Triangle and MLK is at the heart of everything," says Delahunt. "It's connected to many of the shootings in Freeport, Roosevelt, Uniondale, Brooklyn, Queens, Harlem . . . pretty

---

[1] This information is drawn from the author's analysis of police and court records, as well as interviews.

much any neighborhood around here where the Crips and Bloods have a presence. The Triangle's the epicenter, and it radiates out to those other communities in the corridor and out to New York City. No shooting, no drive-by happens in a vacuum. There are repercussions and different moves made in response to every one of them in different neighborhoods, involving different sets and crews.

"The gang world seems simple—he kills my boy, I kill him—but nothing's simple. It's a very tangled web of relationships, of beefs that sometimes go back years and involve all kinds of different gangsters, their associates, their girlfriends, their suppliers, and other hustlers. The deeper you dig, the more craziness you see. Shit, if you dig deep enough, you'll even see the Bloods-Crips connection to the cartels."

CHAPTER TEN

Branching Out

It's what you might call, in the legitimate business world, a volatile market. Every step of the way, there's uncertainty.

—ICE

The Mexicans have come through yet again. The new package they'd sent the Crips is the bomb, Tyrek says, superior to any coke the Triangle pipeheads can recall smoking in Hempstead. A top-notch product needs a name to match, so Tyrek gives it one he figures his crew and customers will appreciate in the run-up to the 2012 presidential election: "Obama."

"Got that Obama," the touts cry from every Crips corner. "Come get that Obama. Shit's White House–pure. Pass me by, you won't get Air Force One high."

Some of the pipeheads, amused by the touts' pitches, begin calling the vials "Air Force Ones" instead of their official name. Whatever they call them, this batch is selling like no product has on these corners in recent years.

Stick-thin addicts, desperate for the stuff, shift nervously in a line that snakes around the corner of Linden Place. Fights break out over who's queued up first. And as profits increase, anger over the murders of Little James and Crazy Ray, as well as Leticia's rape, seems to recede; the mood among the Big Homies now borders on jubilant.

"Money is *right* right now," Tyrek tells Tony and Flex during their weekly meeting to go over the books. "This shit keep up, we going to need to grab some more corners."

The Crips have been talking about a major expansion since before the Triangle war but say the conflict has consumed all their time and energy, keeping them from doing the laborious work of scouting, holding, and staffing large swaths of added territory. Now, with their high-grade coke and a promise from their Mexican suppliers to sell them as much of it as they want, the set is considering a major purchase.

"We put fifty grand of that Obama on the street, we can come back with half a mil," Tyrek says.

"Big investment," Tony says, sounding leery. "Lot of product to stash, lot of risk, especially with the number of police that be creeping right now."

A coke purchase of the magnitude they're now considering could, if the gambit worked, transform the Hempstead Crips from local players into a regional powerhouse. A $50,000 order would give them enough guaranteed-to-move product to open at least two, and possibly three, more corners in central Nassau and New York City. And if the initial expansion succeeded, Tyrek says, they could double their next re-up and extend east into Long Island's more rural half, Suffolk County, where there are still plenty of untapped coke markets.

"This is what we've been wanting since way back," Flex says. "This shit right here goes right? We millionaires, man."

"Millionaires," Tony says, smiling.

Tyrek warns them not to get ahead of themselves. Before they can expand, they must first lay final claim to the territory they're now warring over, defeating the Bloods once and for all, he says. No stalemates. No uncertain terms.

"We've got to obliterate them niggas," Tyrek says.

"No doubt," says Tony.

"But first, go buy us as much of that good new Mexican shit as you can."

Like most well-established Crips and Bloods sets, the Hempstead crews buy their coke and weed from traffickers connected to international drug cartels. The Crips patronize a wholesale supplier in New York City, who, in turn, gets his drugs from a contractor for Mexico's Sinaloa Cartel—the largest, richest, most successful drug-trafficking organization in history. Sinaloa purchases most of its coke from growers in Colombia's mountain-side farms for about $2,000 per kilo—the first step in a highly structured supply chain that allows Sinaloa to export as much as half of all illegal narcotics currently on America's streets.

"From Colombia," says Tony, the Crips' designated expert on drug markets and trends, "that coke package just gets more valuable every step of the way."

The kilo's price rises to about $10,000 in Mexico. After it's smuggled into the United States, its value increases to roughly $30,000. Depending on the quality of an individual cocaine shipment, the Hempstead Crips can buy a kilo for $17,000 to $25,000 from their supplier. Once they have the coke, they turn it into crack inside a series of cookhouses they control in Long Island and Queens. Then they break the crack up into g-packs to sell at retail on the street.

By the time every rock has sold, they've made about $100,000.

"We taking in eighty thousand dollars' profit, give or take a few grand, on every kilo we move," Tony says. "That right there is why crack ain't never going to die. That profit is just too good."

Buyers at each level of the supply chain are not just paying for the drugs. "They're paying for the risks everybody took to get the drugs to that point," Tony says, "which is what drives that price up higher and higher each step of the way."

Corner-dealing crews like those employed by Crips and Bloods prob-ably assume more risk than anyone in the supply chain, standing out in the open in neighborhoods heavily patrolled by police, interacting with strung-out pipeheads, and competing for market share with an enemy crew just blocks away. As a result, the difference between how much they pay for coke versus how much they sell it for is usually significant. They hike up their prices based on the belief that they might be arrested or killed at any moment—and must earn as much money as possible while they're still here. That inflated cost gets passed to street customers, Tony says. And the less competition a crew has in their neighborhoods, the more they can charge.

"In drug markets, like any lucrative markets for illegal goods, there's a ton of pressure driving competitors to try for monopoly," said a high-ranking Drug Enforcement Administration official who's studied the nexus between Latin American drug cartels and African-American street gangs. "The way to achieve monopoly is to destroy the other guy. In the legitimate business world, you can drive a competitor out of business with a number of weapons: predatory pricing, lawsuits, buying them out. But for the drug gangs, violence is pretty much the only way. The situation in the Triangle, when you think about it, is really the result of market forces. Just like the cartel wars in Mexico are about the market."

The carnage wrought by Crips and Bloods can seem tame compared with the Mexican cartel wars south of the border, where the organizations' soldiers are known to murder entire families, behead police officers, and dump decapitated bodies in the streets.

"The Mexican situation looks worse, but when you consider the scale of the damage Crips and Bloods have been causing to individual communities across America for the past half-century, well, the impact's about the same in those neighborhoods," the DEA official says. "Both the cartels and the gangs destroy everything they come near."

Sinaloa isn't overly concerned with the behavior of Crips and Bloods who sell much of their product in America—as long as they help to keep the organization's coffers full, drug investigators say. But that doesn't mean the cartel doesn't keep a close watch on how the gangs do business. In fact, Sinaloa leaders and middle managers read American newspapers and blogs to stay abreast of the havoc wrought by street-level dealers at the bottom of the supply chain, says Pedro Guerrero, a former Sinaloa soldier who helped to manage the cartel's interests in Tijuana and Mexicali for over a decade. Even the cartel's leader, Joaquín Guzmán Loera, known as El Chapo, is kept apprised of what Crips, Bloods, and other American gangs moving Sinaloa product are up to.

"El Chapo respects these street gangs, but thinks they are unnecessarily brutal and bad at doing business in the sense that they bring too much violence to their markets, and violence attracts police," Guerrero says of El Chapo. "Keep in mind, this guy was ordering six murders every day before he had a cup of coffee. And he thinks the Bloods and Crips kill each other too much!"

El Chapo's eventual capture in 2014 would deal a symbolic blow to Sinaloa, but in October 2012, it's the arrest of a different cartel leader, El Chapo's lieutenant, José "El Che" Salgueiro Nevarez, that gets the attention of New York's Bloods and Crips sets.

As one of Sinaloa's logistics and supplies expert, El Che played a significant role in trafficking much of the cocaine and marijuana making its way to Long Island and New York City street gangs, investigators say. In the days following El Che's capture, the Hempstead Crips' main supplier in New York City became so concerned about a delayed drug shipment that he flew to Mexico City for a meeting with his Sinaloa contact. He wanted to know whether El Che's arrest might jeopardize their business arrangement.

"They [cartel leaders] knew there would be a lot of worry after they got El Che, and they wanted to [assure] customers that his capture would not interfere with deliveries or the business they were used to," says Hector Quinones, a former Sinaloa messenger. "To them [Sinaloa senior management], this is a corporation. So just like the top leaders of a big computer or soda company would do if one of the board of directors got arrested and they wanted to calm investors, they sent messengers who talked to all their big customers and said, 'Listen, this is no big deal. It doesn't change our arrangement. Everything will stay exactly as it is, so don't worry.' That's what they told [the supplier] to the Crips in New York."

As some of the largest purveyors of Sinaloa product in America, Crips and Bloods have a huge stake in the narco wars being waged in Mexico. If Sinaloa supply lines are attacked by competing cartels, or law enforcement deals further significant blows to the organization, it can leave the gangs without enough weed, coke, and heroin to meet demand on their corners throughout the United States.

"I read the papers looking at how Sinaloa's doing, because if the Zetas or Juarez Cartel or Knights Templar end up on top, then we might have to find a way to get connected with *their* connect," says Tony, referencing three of Sinaloa's fiercest rivals. "When they got that Sinaloa homie [El Che], I ain't going to lie . . . I was worried. But our connect went down there, got some assurances, and sure enough, everything got back on track soon enough. But, you know, shit changing down there all the time. It's all about who's on top today. Same as out here."

The Bloods, too, get their coke from a city-based trafficker supplied by Sinaloa. In fact, the coke sold on Bloods corners in Hempstead and throughout the corridor usually comes from the same shipment the Crips purchase from.

But differences in the crews' respective products *do* exist. Because they use different chemicals to cut their coke and dilute it to varying degrees, one gang's batch of crack is usually stronger than their competitors. And their suppliers, although both connected to Sinaloa, are not equally reliable. The Crips' wholesaler is rarely late with a delivery. The Bloods' supplier, however, is often delayed with his shipments, and sometimes fails to come up with the full amount ordered. Ice sticks with him only because he has access to some of the highest-quality coke anywhere in New York, and charges the lowest price in town.

"It's what you might call, in the legitimate business world, a volatile market," Ice, the accounting major, says of the drug trade. "Every step of the way, there's uncertainty. In the beginning, we had to find a supplier who could get what we needed and who we could trust. You know how long it took to find that? Two years. For two years, we had to work with smaller dealers, people making promises they could get us more. Then, when they didn't come through, we'd go up the chain to deal directly with the next guy. Eventually, we got in with some good people with Cali connections, through Steed, and we moved up to their main supplier, who was tapped into that good Sinaloa shit.

"That's the ultimate, as far as I'm concerned. We compete with them [other gangs] on quality, and on pricing, too. As someone with a history in the financial world, I take those things seriously. It doesn't matter whether you selling drugs or legal merchandise. The rules of economics and smart business still apply."

Ice says he also has connections to a Dominican supplier in Manhattan, a used-car dealer who works with the Juarez Cartel to smuggle coke from Mexico to the United States. If his current Sinaloa-linked dealer proves unreliable again in the future, Ice says, he might explore doing business with Juarez instead.

"The most important thing in this business is supply," Ice says. "Without that, you ain't got anything else. Territory doesn't matter, your people don't matter, and your strategy don't matter if you ain't got any product coming in."

In Tijuana, men and women who keep America's coke trade humming along the border know all about the Crips and Bloods. Carlos Tomayo, a former driver for Sinaloa, says both gangs' members—mostly from California—are treated like royalty at Mexico's cartel-connected restaurants, hotels, and brothels.

"These black gangsters are the ones who make the cartels rich," says Tomayo. "Without them, the cartels are nothing, because they are the ones who really move the product in America. If there were no Bloods, no Crips, all the other black street gangs would have never been formed. Those two were the first, the biggest, and toughest. They set an example of how you could take drugs brought into the United States and make it a business in their neighborhoods.

"The cartels know all about this. They know that these gangs are their bread and butter. So they respect them. If you are [a Blood or Crip] in Mexico, you are respected by the cartels, by their supporters. Because you are big money to them. You are their connection to the black communities all over America, and white communities, too. Americans love drugs, so the cartels love the gangs who sell it to them."

Tony learns about that love firsthand when he flies to San Diego for his older brother's wedding. He brings along his girlfriend, pregnant with their second son, even though he's worried she'll be uncomfortable traveling. In the end, he decides that leaving her in New York with a gang war raging—and a dozen or so Bloods probably willing to rape or shoot her without a second thought—isn't an option.

The night before the ceremony, Tony, his brother, and five of his brother's friends drive across the border into Tijuana to throw a bachelor party in the city's red-light district. They choose a club recommended by the Crips' coke supplier, who'd given Tony the name of a Sinaloa bigwig he's to mention. Tony's doubtful his role as a player in the suburban New York drug trade will have much of an impression on cartel kingpins or their friends. But once he drops the bigwig's name, the club's staffers give Tony and his party the royal treatment.

They bring out heaping plates of Mexican food and their best beer, mescal, and tequila—enough booze to fell an army. In between food and drinks, they're ushered into upstairs rooms with prostitutes, sometimes several at a time. These are the brothel's most beautiful and sexually "creative" girls, reserved for only the most distinguished visitors, Tony is assured by the club manager, a man named Federico.

"You are—and tell me if I'm saying this right—one of the Creeps?" he asks Tony amid the festivities. "We are great admirers of yours."

"Crips," Tony says, laughing at his host's pronunciation. "I guess you all don't see us New York hustlers down here too often."

"Not often, no," Federico says. "But believe me when I say, my bosses are very grateful for your business, and wish to ensure all your needs are met while you're in Tijuana."

As Tony's party grows more boisterous, lighting up blunts and grabbing the backsides of waitresses as they pass, some of the cartel soldiers in the club shake their heads at them. The crudeness, gluttony, and lack of refinement on display disgusts them. Where do these animals get off, fucking our women, drinking our booze, they wonder? How come they're being served at all in this establishment, much less treated so well? But when these men complain to Federico, each of them is scolded in turn, told to shut up and mind their own business.

"If you don't understand how important these men are to us," Federico says to one of the disgruntled soldiers, "then you are dumber than you look."

Tony has no idea what the soldiers think of him and his gang brothers back home—that they're fools and thugs of the worst kind, low-class criminals who enslave their own people to crack. All Tony knows is that the bosses of these men must appreciate the Crips' business and respect what they do. The drug business, after all, is all about respect, Tony says: who gets it, who gives it, and how it's earned. It's something anyone in the drug game—a nightclub owner from Tijuana or a Crip from Long Island—can understand.

"At the end of the day, we all speak this same language," Tony says. "Language of respect, language of the street."

Back at his brother's house, once he's showered and washed the smell of prostitutes off him, Tony climbs into bed beside his girlfriend, kisses her belly, and whispers a greeting to his unborn son. The boy, he hopes, will speak this language, too.

CHAPTER ELEVEN

Basic Training

I'm part of this thing now. Whether I want to be or not.

—DEVON

Back in the Triangle, a pair of detectives stands over the body of Doc Reed, pondering the piece of scalp missing from his head. It lay beside a storm drain, ten feet from his corpse. "What do you think did that—a .45?"

"Nah, .357."

"No way."

"Twenty bucks says I'm right," one detective says, both of them clearly desensitized by now to the horrors of life in a war zone.

"Make it fifty."

"Doc, if I lose this bet, I'm blaming you," the detective says, addressing the corpse.

After narrowly surviving the nine-millimeter slug Dice Beckles had shot through his stomach in January, Doc's luck has finally run out. Dice had spotted him waiting in line at a nearby McDonald's drive-through in Freeport earlier that afternoon and had followed him back to a Bloods cookhouse a few blocks south of the Mercedes service center. Dice blew half his head off as Doc walked up to the door, bag full of quarter-pounders still in hand.

"If he hadn't stopped for them burgers, he'd still be alive," Dice says.

Their months-long feud, for all the bloodshed it has caused, originated with nothing more than a funny look.

"I didn't like the way he stared at me when he rolled past one night," says Dice. "So the next day, I shot him. But he ain't die. Then he tried to shoot *me*. But he killed Little James instead. So I *had* to do his ass when I saw him at the drive-through."

Doc's killing stuns the Bloods, who are still reeling from the murder of Big Mac, the shootings of Steed and Spider Rick, and the attack on Ice's sister. Doc's death also creates an immediate opening for a corner supervisor, which Ice orders Tony to fill as quickly as possible. After considering a handful of candidates, they settle on Devon LaFleur.

"D-Bo," as he's known to his friends, is seventeen, six-foot-one, and muscular, a good student who recently began selling weed for the Bloods on weekends in order to make more money to spend on his girlfriend, Shonda. He'd initially tried his hand at two legitimate after-school jobs—first, as a clerk at CVS, and later, at Dunkin' Donuts. But the pay of $8 to $9 an hour amounted to so little after taxes, Devon could barely afford a nice dinner date once a week.

"I'm tired of being broke," he told Shonda one afternoon as they walked through Roosevelt Field Mall in Garden City, an upscale shopping center a short drive from the Triangle. Garden City is Hempstead's wealthier, almost exclusively white neighborhood to the north, a place close on the map yet worlds apart in every other way.

"If you so broke, do something about it," Shonda said. "Show me what you're all about."

Devon upped his earnings by taking the weekend dealing gig with the Bloods but could barely keep up with Shonda's requests for food and gifts. Unhappy with his progress, she broke up with him. A short time later, he spotted her walking through the mall, hand in hand with a Crips Big Homie from Brooklyn, Christian Louboutin shoes on her feet and new diamond studs in her ears.

Crushed by the sight, Devon vowed to get Shonda back by bringing in some "real money." No more low-wage jobs making breakfast sandwiches or stocking shelves. No more scrounging up a few dollars from nickel-bag weed sales just to take his girl to a movie.

"Yo, you need somebody full-time right now?" Devon asked Steed one Saturday, after his shift ended. "I need more dollars, for real."

Steed was delighted by the job inquiry. He'd known Devon since the kid was in elementary school and had always liked him, despite the fact that D-Bo never got blunted with the Bloods when invited. Even as his classmates gravitated toward the gangs controlling their neighborhood, Devon kept straight—no banging, no fighting, no drugs. Partying and drama didn't seem to suit him. Steed thought such discipline would make him a good replacement for Doc.

"Yeah, homie, I got more work for you," Steed said. "Come 'round tomorrow night and I'll get you started."

That was all it took.

A month later and Devon knows the ins and outs of the Bloods dealing operation so thoroughly, he's running the MLK shop as smoothly as his deceased predecessor. Steed's thrilled with his progress, and when he suggests to Ice that they make Devon a full-fledged Blood, the gang leader embraces the idea.

"That boy's a worker, so we going to work him," Ice says. "We need good soldiers right about now."

But when Steed offers Devon official membership, the boy is caught off guard. Devon explains that he's got a B average in school—not great, but better than his colleagues on the corner, and good enough to get him into a four-year college should he come up with the tuition money. If he goes to college as a Blood, he wonders, what will be expected of him? Will he be asked to sling to classmates? Will Steed and Ice give him time off to attend classes?

"Nigga, we'll work all that shit out," Steed says. "We want you to be part of our family. This here's an honor. That's how you should be looking at it."

There are good reasons for officially joining, too, Devon knows. It would ensure the continuance of his job as corner supervisor and allow him to keep getting paid like he has been these last two months. The money's been right, even better than he'd expected when Steed took him on full-time. He's making about $800 a week, plus the $100 to $200 end-of-month bonuses Steed throws him for his good work. His original plan was to run the corner just long enough to save two or three grand, then knock on Shonda's door holding a fat stack of cash. Now, he has all but forgotten about her. Shifting rationales are common in the Triangle, where young men often enter the drug game vowing a temporary stint, but get sucked in permanently by the easy money, street fame, and sense of power granted them through membership.

There are new, prettier girls hanging with Devon since he gained access to all that good coke and weed. And his stature in the neighborhood has soared since word got around about his corner savvy, his glowing reputation making him all the more attractive to the ladies. He takes one or two of them out every week for steaks at Ruth's Chris or for lobsters on the pier in Port Jefferson. It doesn't bother Devon that they never so much as looked at him before he started slinging. All that matters is that he's a player now, and he loves the way it feels.

With so much cash coming in, he can barely find enough ways to spend it. Every weekend, he hits up the mall and splurges on new gear: Air Jordans and Timberland shoes, Tom Ford shirts, Ralph Lauren jackets, Gucci sunglasses, Armani *everything*. With bankrolls this thick, how can he walk away?

To sweeten the deal, Tony says, Ice will even help Devon with SAT prep and pay for his college tuition, wanting the young man to excel in the classroom as well as on the corner. As the only local gangster with a college degree, Ice still believes in helping his employees sharpen their minds—even if it means they might one day leave the business in search of something better.

"All right," Devon says, accepting the membership offer. "Let's do this."

"That's good to hear," Steed says. "Proud of you, yo."

An initiation ceremony is scheduled for the following week, with Devon given a night off for the occasion. At the designated time, a dozen Bloods gather in a dark corner of Campbell Park, which sits in the shadow of Hempstead's baby-blue water tower.

Pictured here, some Crips and prayer marchers walk past Campbell Park and Hempstead's water tower. The park is where Devon LaFleur, a local student, is "jumped in" as part of his initiation into the Bloods during the gang war.
STEVE PFOST

Most of the gangsters are drunk or high off the bottles of beer and blunts they pass to one another. All seem excited by the sanctioned opportunity to clobber one of their own.

After a few minutes, Steed calls them to attention and they form a circle. "Thirty seconds," he says. "I got the count."

Someone pushes Devon into the middle of the circle, and before he can get his balance, the gangsters are upon him. Their punches come in flurries, some thrown half-assed and landing soft, others thrown with weight behind them, crashing into his face and body with such force they steal his breath. His lip is busted open by one blow from "Super" Curt Ellis, his nose bloodied by another from James "J-Roc" Pendleton. Doubled over, he takes a kick to the stomach and a left hook to the side of his head; then a right hook; then another left.

"Twenty-five," Steed says, marking the seconds left in the initiation.

The punches rain down on Devon's face, arms, and back until, finally, he's angry enough to fight back. He swings wildly but only catches air at first. Then he lands a punch on Big Boy Owens's lip, wheels around, and pounds Super Curt on the ear with a straight right.

"Twenty," Steed says.

Devon stops swinging long enough to catch his breath and some-one—he doesn't see who—clocks him hard in the back of his head. He stumbles forward, his momentum carrying him toward Steed, who puts his arms out as if to catch his prized pupil. But at the last moment, he rears back and swings at Devon, his knuckles smashing against his right eye. The blow makes a cracking sound that seems to excite the others.

"Hells yeah," Big Boy says. "Got his ass good."

"Nigga got dropped," says J-Roc, laughing.

"Fifteen," Steed says, Devon crumpled at his feet.

Some of the Bloods help him up, only to push him back into the middle of the circle. He sways, his legs feeling like rubber, before righting himself. He lifts his hands in a boxer's pose.

"He's a soldier," J-Roc says.

"Boy got heart," says Steed.

Big Boy gets a running start and lands a right hook on Devon's already-swollen right eye. He follows up with an uppercut to Devon's chin and a straight right to his nose. Devon tries to counter with a right hook but misses, creating an opening for Big Boy to land a series of uppercuts to his stomach. One, two, three punches crash into his belly as he gasps for air.

"Ten seconds," Steed says.

They all join in the countdown then, shouting out numbers as they pile on Devon, landing blow after blow.

"Nine! Eight! Seven!"

J-Roc lands a hard left on Devon's cheek, opening a fresh cut. Some of the boys ease up then, seeing their new inductee's taken a severe beating with time nearly up. But others stay on him, like Big Boy, who pounds his nose with a straight right hand, followed by a left to his busted cheek.

"Six! Five! Four!"

Devon struggles to stay on his feet, lurching from side to side as J-Roc comes up from his rear, lifts him in the air, and body-slams him on the grass. Super Curt kicks him in his side a few times, and some of the other Bloods join him, getting in their last licks. Devon pulls himself into a ball, trying to shrink their target.

"Three! Two! One!"

Just before time is called, Big Boy gets a good head of steam and gives a soccer-style kick to Devon's crotch, eliciting a long whimper.

"Done," says Steed.

They let him lay there a minute or two before helping him up, hugging him, and offering their congratulations.

"Now you with us for life, yo," Big Boy says. "No matter where you go, you got family right here. Like blood."

"Boy, you took a licking and kept on ticking," Steed says, handing Devon his official Bloods kerchief. "You proved today you belong. Anything you need from now on, you come to me. We family now. You feel me?"

Devon nods his head, afraid to open his mouth because of the blood he feels splashing around behind his teeth. Later, when he walks in the door at home, his mother cries at the sight of his bruised, bloodied face. The sound of her sobbing carries up MLK for a long while, even after Devon's gone to bed.

—◆—

Despite his mother's pleas, Devon's on the corner the next afternoon, his right eye swollen shut, his face and body covered in cuts and welts.

"You can handle anything after what we put you through," Steed tells him. "Now you a man for real. Nothing going to faze you."

"I ain't ever seen these boys get after one of our niggas like that," Super Curt says. "You took everything they had. Mad respect, yo."

"Thanks," Devon mumbles, struggling to get the words out through bruised lips.

"Since you done so good, I'm giving you a raise," Steed says. "Taking you up to nine hundred a week, plus the monthly bonus. So you going to have plenty to spend on them hos you be taking out all the time."

Steed drives off then and leaves Devon to run the MLK shop. Business is brisk, and his corner crew sells out their g-pack by lunchtime. Devon calls for a re-up, and half of *that* package sells out by the end of the after-work rush.

"We putting in work today," he tells the crew, his mouth starting to feel a little better. "You all doing good."

Devon is counting up the midday proceeds when a silver Acura rolls past, its occupants staring hard at him. He recognizes them as Crips, figures that word must have gotten around to the Triangle that he's official now. He hadn't thought much about the gang war before joining the Bloods, believing he could leave all that beefing to the others. He used to be friends with a few Crips, after all, even tutoring Bolo Jay in math after school.

The Acura's front-seat passenger, Flex Butler, is another childhood friend of Devon's. But there is only hatred in his eyes now as he rolls by, whistling loudly at D-Bo. When he's sure he's got his attention, Flex extends his right hand out the window, bends it into the shape of a gun, closes one eye, and mimes pulling the trigger.

"Boom!" Flex says, laughing, the Acura speeding off.

Devon thinks of Little James then, remembering a photo of his corpse Doc had taken with his iPhone after the killing and proudly showed off. The image captured the back of James's head, blood leaking out of his skull beneath a Knicks cap, his eyes still open.

Devon wonders how long it will be before there's another murder.

"I'm part of this thing now," Devon says once the Acura's out of sight. "Whether I want to be or not."

CHAPTER TWELVE

Battle Scars

If you a soldier, it don't matter whether you fighting in your own hood or in the Middle East. A soldier's a soldier wherever he's at.

—Flex

Mike Clary, a Triangle resident, marine, and Iraq War vet who served three tours, can't sleep more than a few hours without being awakened by gunplay or nightmares. Tonight, a cacophony of shots and screams along Linden Avenue mingle with the roar in his mind of insurgent mortar fire and exploding roadside bombs in Fallujah. He wakes in a cold sweat, screaming into his dark, empty bedroom. It seems neither war—the one he fought in the desert, nor the one being waged outside his door—will let him be.

He checks the clock and sees it's two a.m. Too late to call his wife, Diane, he knows, but he dials her number anyway, hoping she'll answer and talk him through this latest flashback. Even as her line rings, Clary feels as if he's back with his doomed convoy: the shrapnel again piercing his neck, back, buttocks, and legs; the flames again engulfing his body in a shroud of agonizing heat. Memories of the IED attack sweep over him two or three time a day, each episode as vivid as the ambush itself in Fallujah. He'd refused to see a mental health professional for two years after his return, despite Diane's constant pleas and willingness to see him through his recovery. Month after month, he resisted her efforts, discarding psychiatry as "a scam" while failing to acknowledge the extent of his illness.

"Whatever's going on in my head will take care of itself," he'd say.

Some nights he'd wake up howling in pain beside his wife, feeling again the fire that had consumed the entire back of his body and forced him to undergo more than ten surgeries at the US military hospital in Ramstein, Germany. Diane would hold him when he awakened, whispering that it would all be all right, that he was safe at home. He'd often shove her away, believing she was attacking rather than comforting him.

"Tell your doctors at the VA you have PTSD," she ordered him one day, a little over a year after his return. "Otherwise I'm leaving. Today."

"I don't need anyone messing with my head," he said. "If you don't like it, do what you got to do."

And just like that, she was gone.

Eight months later, Clary's ready to admit he was wrong. He's ready to accept the support and care Diane offered him so often, which he rejected, sometimes violently. He's seeing a VA psychiatrist twice weekly—treatment mandated by a judge following a recent arrest for public intoxication. The doctor has helped him to understand that post-traumatic stress disorder is nothing to be ashamed of. Many of the men he served with also suffer from it.

He wants to tell all this to Diane, if only she'd pick up.

"I'm getting help," he says on her answering machine for the hundredth time. "Please call me. I need you."

But he doesn't really believe she'll come back. Not after what he'd done to her, bloodying her lip several times when she'd awakened him in the middle of his nightmares. Other times, when she'd tried to embrace him during his flashbacks, he'd thrown her to the ground. She might have forgiven all of those things, too, if he'd been willing to move out of the Triangle. He'd grown up in his parents' house there and never left, believing the neighborhood would one day gentrify—that the house would eventually double or triple in value. He'd hoped to pass the property along to their children, if they ever had any, as an asset.

But in the two years they'd been married before he shipped off to Iraq for the first time, the violence surrounding their home had only intensified.

"It's like it's not even America," Diane wrote him in an e-mail while he was overseas. "In the Triangle, it's like a Third World country."

When Clary came home, Diane saw how gunplay in the neighborhood affected him. She begged him to move to another community. If he wouldn't see a psychiatrist, she said, giving them a change of scenery was the least he could do.

"I'm not moving," Clary said each time she brought it up. "These fucking gangbangers are the ones who should be moving. Not us."

Now, his combat flashback receding, Clary hears voices in the street. He looks through a slit in the blinds of his bedroom window to see what the gangsters are up to. They're drinking bottled beer in the middle of the block, smoking blunts in plain sight as though they're kings, the Triangle their kingdom. Clary, knowing he won't be able to sleep amid the noise, puts on a T-shirt, shorts, and slippers before heading for the front door.

Somebody's got to give some straight talk to these knuckleheads, he thinks.

He's been thinking about this moment for a long time—the moment when he might make a stand against these kids, while also helping them see the wastes they're making of their lives. He wishes someone had done the same thing for him when he was a kid in Hempstead, snatching purses and boosting cars. His hand on the doorknob, Clary stops for a moment, considering whether he should grab the Smith & Wesson pistol in his nightstand drawer. He decides against it, figuring that whatever else he does with the rest of his life, killing won't be a part of it. Not after what he'd seen and done in Iraq.

He takes a deep breath, puffs out his chest, and steps outside.

"Y'all need to keep it down out here," Clary tells the Crips standing in the street. "People are trying to sleep. Just take the volume down a notch or two, please."

The Crips—Tyrek, Tony, Flex, Rock, and Savant—take stock of the slipper-clad, light-skinned black man, then bust out laughing. They're partying tonight to observe the six-month anniversary of Little James's death. No way this fool's going to keep them from a good time.

"Is this mulatto nigga serious?" Tony says. "Yo, go back inside your house, old man, before you get hurt."

Clary doesn't budge. He's stared down al-Qaeda fighters ten times as tough as these idiots. They're the ones who should be inside at this hour.

"You deaf?" Tony says. "I said get the fuck in your house."

"Son, I've got to ask you to show some respect," Clary says, knowing there's no turning back now. "Not just for me, but for the families on this block with children who are trying to sleep. It's hard to rest with all the noise y'all are making out here. It's a school night. Just be mindful of that."

Tony smiles, nods his head as if in sympathy. He sucks down the rest of his beer and, without warning, fires the bottle at Clary's head. The marine doesn't see it coming in time. He takes the full force of it on his mouth, hears a tooth chip, feels the glass shatter and slice his bottom lip. But the pain doesn't alarm him. Not in the least. He's felt plenty worse.

"We ain't playing with you, nigga," Tony says. "I told you go back inside or you was going to get hurt. You see what you done brought on yourself?"

Clary spits out a blood-soaked piece of tooth, looking the boys directly in their eyes. In his bloodstained shirt, veins popping out of his neck and forehead, he's a scary sight. At least, that's what he hopes, given that he's left his pistol inside.

"You trying to be Rambo or some shit?" Tyrek says. " 'Cause you in a dangerous situation right here."

"I did three tours in Iraq while you were out here playing gangster," Clary says. "Fuck you know about dangerous?"

Clary had meant to keep his cool when he came out here. He'd told himself he'd be the bigger man, the adult, no matter how badly the gangsters goaded him. He'd show them he wasn't afraid; in doing so, he'd gain their respect and make a connection. Then he'd give them some straight talk, explain that there are better ways to live than dealing drugs and shooting each other. But now he has lost his temper, and with it, any chance he might have had at relating to these kids.

"Oh, nigga's a war veteran," Tyrek says mockingly. "Went chasing after Saddam and shit."

"Look, I ain't looking for a fight," Clary says, the adrenaline leaving him now. "I didn't mean you no disrespect. I just wanted to level with—"

Before Clary can finish his sentence, Tyrek lands a haymaker on his right eye. The blow knocks him to the pavement, his head smashing into the street with a sickening thud. Tyrek shakes his hand, which is already beginning to swell, and steps over the knocked-out marine. He bends down and gives Clary's cheek a little slap, wanting to make sure he's not dead. Killing an enemy gangster with his bare fist would be a triumph for the Crips leader, but cutting down a noncombatant this way—a war veteran, no less—would draw all kinds of heat from the cops. After another few slaps, each one harder than the next, Clary moves his head a little. Tyrek exhales, relieved to know he won't have another homicide probe to worry about.

The Crips, in a gesture they'd never make to a true foe, call for an ambulance before sauntering off.

"Yeah, keep leveling," Tyrek mumbles, sucking on his bruised knuckles.

—◆—

Later, Clary's in a bed at Nassau University Medical Center, an intravenous painkiller drip beside him. He eyes the medical equipment in the room, recalling from his days in Germany what each gadget tracks, how each works its magic on a broken body.

"Feels like old times," he says.

Diagnosed with a concussion, Clary's released the next day. He catches a taxi home and, as he exits the cab, sees Devon LaFleur barking out orders to some hustlers up the street near MLK. The kid sure has changed, Clary thinks. He remembers seeing Devon around the neighborhood, a hardworking, well-behaved teen, kind and respectful in all of their interactions. He'd seemed to effortlessly navigate the dual elements of the neighborhood—the hustlers and the industrious strivers—without fully giving himself over to either. Now, the kid's wearing a Boston Red Sox cap emblazoned with the trademark B—a favorite among Bloods members—and appears to be delegating responsibilities to a corner drug crew.

"Hey, D-Bo, what's the good word, my man?" Clary says, crossing the street to greet Devon. The rest of the Bloods glare at the interloper, but Devon offers him a big smile.

"Mr. Clary, welcome home, sir."

Still got his manners, Clary thinks, despite the fact he's running with these fools. Devon flashes a "timeout" signal to his crew and shakes Clary's hand.

"Surprised to see you out here, son. Your mother know about this?"

Devon looks back at the hustlers, tells them he'll be right back. He leads Clary up the block so the boys can't hear their conversation.

"Yeah, she knows. She don't like it none."

"Psshh. I don't imagine she does. How'd you get involved with these knuckleheads?"

Under the streetlights, Clary gets his first up-close look at Devon's face. He seems to have aged a decade since their last talk three years earlier, with blue bags and bruises beneath his eyes, patches of gray hairs crawling up his sideburns. The Triangle has done a number on him, Clary thinks.

Clary doesn't look too good himself, with a fresh stitch in his lip and a bandage wrapped around his swollen head. Devon had heard about the beatdown, but spares Clary the embarrassment of mentioning it.

"I'm just putting in work," Devon says. "Nothing more than that."

"Boy, don't give me that 'It's just a job' routine," says Clary, angry that such a good kid—in his mind, the smartest one in the neighborhood—is out here slinging vials. "Those Crips liable to come shoot up this corner anytime."

"I know," Devon says. "But I'm just trying to make a little something for myself. I ain't involved in any of this other stuff."

"By other stuff, you mean boys getting their domes blown off?" Clary says.

"Yo, D-Bo, Steed calling for you," one of the Bloods interrupts. "He says you need to get with him at PL[1] right now."

"Aight, tell him I'll be right there," Devon says.

"Steed Wallace," says Clary. "You done got yourself involved with some nasty characters, son."

---

[1] Park Lake apartments

"I got to go," Devon says, giving Clary a parting handshake before starting toward Park Lake. "See you around."

"Yo, D-Bo," Clary says. "Remember to keep your head up."

"I will."

Walking back to his house, Clary notices a few Crips watching him from a stoop on Linden Avenue. Tony's there. So is Tyrek, pressing a bag full of ice cubes against his fist. Unbeknownst to Clary, they're in the middle of formulating a final assault on the Bloods—an attack they hope will decisively end the Triangle conflict.

Clary returns their gaze and nods, as if to say "No hard feelings." Tyrek, after a few moments, nods back.

"Nigga's got balls," Tony says.

"Got to respect a player who get right back up," says Tyrek.

"Yeah, but we should *still* cap his ass if he pull that Rambo shit again."

"Shit. That goes without saying."

On the other side of the Triangle, Ice is chewing on his fingernails between long sips of Hennessy, thinking about Doc's murder. He knows Tyrek's people are moving against his crew, targeting Bloods' relatives, pushing them closer to defeat as September draws to a close. And he's unsure how to respond.

He takes a call from his aunt Cheryl, an ordained minister in Atlanta and Ice's only real connection to his pre-dealing life. Cheryl hadn't given up on him, even after it became clear he'd chosen to make a career out of being a criminal. She's long encouraged Ice to move to Atlanta for a fresh start, and she tries again now, sensing Francine's rape and overdose is connected to her brother's drug business.

"Come live with us," Cheryl says. "It'll be a new beginning for you. I get the feeling you're up to your neck in it out there."

Atlanta gives all kinds of breaks to small business owners, she tells him. Why doesn't he start a little accounting firm out here? She and her husband have money they can loan him to get it up and running—not that he needs it, with all those corners he's running. Maybe he could rent some office space downtown in Atlanta's commercial district, get involved with the chamber of commerce. He'd always been such a smart kid, such a savvy businessman.

"I know you can do big things, Michael," Cheryl says.

"I *am* doing big things," says Ice.

"But not in the way you ought to be."

Ice remembers sitting on Cheryl's lap as a child, laughing as she sang nursery rhymes and bounced him on her knee. His mother was already dabbling with the pipe then, and his father, the leader of a Bloods set in Washington Heights, had been shot to death three months after his birth. Cheryl—unlike her sister, Ice's mother—had made good and escaped Hempstead. She'd married one of Atlanta's most successful black businessmen. Together, they owned a string of popular stores in the city and its suburbs and would fly Ice and his mother into Georgia for weeklong visits when Ice was a small child.

"I'm a businessman, Auntie," Ice says. "Same as your man."

"My man is not selling drugs," says Cheryl. "There's a big difference."

"Not that big," Ice says. "Business is business."

"You're dealing the stuff that got your sister killed," Cheryl says. "Don't tell me that's even close to a legitimate business, boy."

"My people don't sell no heroin."

"Right, they just serve up those rocks, because they're harmless. They never hurt a soul. Least of all, your mother."

Ice is silent on that point. He hasn't seen his mother in two years, having cut her off after she continued to blow all the money he gave her on crack. She'd been on and off the pipe since Ice's father died but picked it up full-time when Ice started making real money with the Bloods. At first, she used the cash he gave her for rent and groceries to buy rock from Ice's own corner dealers. When he found out, he stuck Big Mac on the offending dealers and told his mom he was finished with her. Now, she gets her drugs from the Crips.

"That woman got nothing to do with me," Ice says. "She's been cut off a long time now."

"Your mother might be lost to us, I know," Cheryl says. "And Francine's gone. But I'm not giving up on you, Michael. I can't lose you, too."

"I ain't lost," Ice says. "I'm doing good, Auntie. I work for myself . . . don't answer to any fools the way I had to at my other jobs. I got people on my payroll with families, with kids, and they get taken care of behind what we do out here. You may not like it, but it's work. It's business."

"Business, huh?" Cheryl says. "Well, I call it what it is—a racket. A racket that turns folks into junkies and gets them killed. People in your own family, Michael. Your own sister got *raped*—she *died* over some gang nonsense you're mixed up with. Can't you see that?"

"Yeah, I see that," he says. "I see that she was weak, that she couldn't handle the game. Can't say I fault her on that. The game be rough."

"You sound like a fool," Cheryl says. "You can make something of your life, something real. But you got to do it soon, before the game catches up with you."

Ice wonders how hard it would be to take her advice—to pack a bag, hand the reins of the set to Steed, and get on a plane to Atlanta. He knows Tyrek has him on the ropes here, knows the constant threat of assassination has warped his mind in some irreversible way. If only he could get away from it all, maybe go back for his master's degree in finance, maybe read all those books he still hasn't gotten around to. But it's just a pipe dream, he knows. The war is still waiting outside his door.

"The game's going to catch up, regardless; that's the game," Ice says. "Love you, Auntie."

Ice hangs up the phone. He pours himself another Hennessy and stares out the window, watching one of his corner crews work the evening rush. Most wear bulletproof vests under their shirts now, always on alert for a Crips drive-by.

"Soldiers," Ice says, admiring their commitment.

The action of the drug corner once seemed hypnotic to Ice, even soothing. He'd long found comfort in the rhythms of the market; in watching his dealers make hand-to-hand sales with ease and fluidity; in surveying the flow of cars stopping to score. He'd recognized an almost meditative quality in those rituals.

But lately, it all seems ominous to him, the rhythms of the corner foreboding rather than comforting. Ice doesn't know when the change began, or why, but it's intensifying every day. Now, as an old Honda Civic pulls up to the corner, he again experiences that crawling sense of dread, growing stronger as a Bloods tout scrambles over to take the driver's order. Ice studies the wheelman's face and thinks he recognizes him as a Crips associate, a crazy, buck-toothed fool named Marvin who'd shot Ice in the leg seven years earlier, giving him his limp.

Just then a boom—a shotgun blast, Ice thinks—is heard in the street below. A cloud of smoke appears near the beat-up Civic. Ice drops to the carpet, gets on his belly, and covers his head. An ambush, he thinks. Marvin probably took out Ice's tout with that first shot and is on his way upstairs. Ice knows he should go grab one of the guns he has hidden throughout the apartment, but he's paralyzed by fear—a crippling anxiety that sets his hands trembling and makes him certain he's about to die. Marvin will burst in any second now and blow his head off, he's sure.

Ice hears more shots fired in the stairwell, followed by screaming in the hallway just outside his apartment. The smell of gunpowder fills his nostrils. He hears banging on the door, the sound of boot heels kicking it again and again, followed by the crack of splintering wood. It's almost the end, Ice thinks, beginning to pray. He'll be with Francine soon, with Mac, Lamar, and Doc.

Five minutes later, there's nothing but silence. Ice risks a peek at the door. Still locked and chained. No one has kicked it in. He steadies his hands, takes a few deep breaths, and steals a quick look out the window. The street's empty except for a Bloods tout. The old Civic is gone, no trace of it but for a bit of smoke and the smell of oil. It was just a car backfiring. Not a shotgun blast.

He looks farther up the block and sees a guy peering under the hood of the broken-down, smoking car. He's fifty-something with graying hair. Just a middle-aged pipehead, slightly buck-toothed. Marvin's daddy, maybe, but definitely not Marvin. *What the fuck is wrong with me?* Ice thinks.

He has been having these episodes for weeks now—bouts of intense fear set off by a loud noise, familiar face, or something else that calls to mind one of the violent acts he'd witnessed or participated in over the years. He wonders if it's the same thing that marine over in the Triangle's been dealing with since coming home from Iraq. Everybody says the war made him crazy, that he wakes up neighbors with his screaming in the middle of the night. PTSD, they call it. Ice has never been overseas, but he's seen plenty of death, plenty of boys getting blown apart. He wonders if someone can get PTSD from gangbanging. If they can, he thinks, just about every soldier out here must have it.

"There ain't no VA for gangsters, though," he says.

His self-diagnosis may be spot-on. Americans who suffer traumatic injuries like gunshot wounds develop PTSD about as frequently as war veterans like Clary, studies have found. Just like their counterparts in the armed forces, nonveteran trauma victims can experience lifelike night-mares, paranoia, flashbacks, explosive anger, and withdrawal from their families and friends. But efforts to recognize and treat PTSD outside the military are in their infancy. In high-crime, impoverished, mostly black neighborhoods like the Triangle, hardly any efforts are made at all.

The young men wounded by gunfire and stabbings here and in scores of gang-plagued communities throughout America aren't getting treatment for PTSD, research shows. In fact, they're not even close to being diagnosed, since few have access to affordable mental health care, and according to many gang members, the stigma associated with anxiety, depression, and other psychiatric issues in their social circles remains strong.

Recent studies show that about 8 percent of all Americans suffer from PTSD at some point, but that number is significantly higher—as much as 30 to 42 percent, by some estimates—in communities where gang violence is prevalent. In one study, researchers at Chicago's Cook County Hospital found that 42 percent of 307 shooting, stabbing, and other trauma victims surveyed in 2011 exhibited symptoms of PTSD.

In a separate, Atlanta-based study, researchers interviewed more than 8,000 inner-city residents and found roughly two-thirds of them had been violently attacked. About half of them said they personally knew someone who'd become a murder victim. And at least a third of them experienced symptoms consistent with PTSD at some point in their lives—a "conservative estimate," the project's lead investigator, Dr. Kerry Ressler, told ProPublica.

"The rates of PTSD we see are as high, or higher than, Iraq, Afghanistan, or Vietnam veterans," Ressler said. "We have a whole population who is traumatized."

In the Triangle and other New York communities plagued by Crips and Bloods violence, that trauma is painfully obvious. A survey of ninety-seven people wounded by gunfire during the past fifteen years in Hempstead, Uniondale, Freeport, Roosevelt, and Queens found that about 60 percent of them showed signs of PTSD.[2] Sixty-five of them self-identify as Crips, Bloods, or their affiliates. Among them: Ice, Steed, Tyrek, Tony, and Flex, all of whom were wounded by gunfire at some point. The fact that none received an official diagnosis or treatment for PTSD—and continued to perpetrate violence against others after being wounded—is probably not coincidental, research indicates.

"Neglect of civilian PTSD as a public health concern may be compromising public safety" because some untreated sufferers tend to commit violent acts, Ressler and his research team found.

Clary, unlike the gangsters he shares a neighborhood with, suffered his emotional trauma while serving his country. He was nearly killed by an IED, saw a friend's head blown off by a sniper, and watched as the limbs of several marines were shredded by roadside bombs. He'd also killed an insurgent at close range, he said, "something that ensured I'd never kill again, because of the weight it put on me."

As a result of the carnage he's witnessed, Clary finds himself constantly bracing for possible attack, living every moment in a hypervigilant state. He'd brought those behaviors home from Iraq, and the gang violence in the streets only exacerbated them, his doctors said.

"I'm always expecting something horrible to happen," he says.

Clary and Hempstead Crips and Bloods speak in remarkably similar terms about their symptoms, even though most gang members have never set foot outside the state of New York, much less fought overseas.

---

[2] Data is drawn from the author's survey of gunshot victims on Long Island.

"Ever since the times I got shot and shot at, I don't see like I used to," says Tyrek, who has survived several gunshot wounds. "Afterward, I saw everything like a hawk, man, like every detail mattered because my life depended on me not missing nothing. And the same went for my hearing. I heard, like, *every* little thing, because you've got to listen for footsteps coming up behind you, for Bloods who be creeping. It's like I had some kind of antennae that went way up and been there ever since. I don't know what you call that, medically. I call that staying alive. I mean, if my body and my brain telling me I'm in danger, even if there ain't no danger at that time, I don't see that as a bad thing. Because at some point, the danger's going to be real. And I need to be ready for it, or I'm dead."

In Flex's opinion, there's no difference between being at war in an overseas combat zone and fighting Bloods in his hometown. So it shouldn't come as a surprise, he says, that PTSD symptoms experienced by many veterans after they return home are the same ones plaguing some gangsters.

"If you a soldier, it don't matter whether you fighting in your own hood or in the Middle East," Flex says. "A soldier's a soldier wherever he's at. All that shit about mental illnesses or whatever? That's bullshit, yo. Ain't no illness. Ain't nothing you can do to fix those kinds of thoughts. It's just soldiering. You live with it, or you get out the game. Always going to be that way, whatever a doctor says about it."

The only Triangle or MLK resident to receive an official diagnosis of PTSD other than Clary is Donna Crawford, who lost two sons—and more recently, her nephew Lamar—to gang shootings.

"These scars on the mind are real," she says. "And they last forever."

CHAPTER THIRTEEN

Trojan Horse

Halfway gets you killed or gets you caught.

—Ice

The war's end is near, Tyrek says on Halloween night. No more tit-for-tat shootings with the Bloods. No more half-measures. Tonight, he's putting his plan to end the Triangle conflict into motion.

"This plan," he says, "is some David Petraeus–type shit."

He has just sent out word of his desire to negotiate a truce with the Bloods, a cease-fire that will allow both sets to get on with their business. No more killings or rapes, he has promised. No more extra heat from the cops.

Of course, it's all a ruse designed to get close to Bloods leaders and take them out. But Ice and his men don't know that.

When Tyrek dispatches Tony to convince the Bloods of the offer's legitimacy, they're leery.

"I'm relating to you what my man Tyrek is promising," he tells the small cadre of enemy gangsters led by Steed, who have agreed, with serious reservations, to meet with Tony in the old DMZ outside Marsha Ricks's home. "Tyrek wants peace."

Steed tells Tony he finds it hard to believe Tyrek's willing to end the war, or agree to any territorial concessions. After all, there had been rumors of a proposed truce at the start of the year, which the Crips swiftly quashed. Tony tries to allay their concerns now, insisting Tyrek wouldn't have sent him to negotiate if he weren't serious.

"He knows you all could pop me right here, and that would be all the answer he needs," Tony says. "But he also knows sending me here's a show of good faith. Means he thinks we can talk about this shit like men instead of doing like we been doing."

The Bloods stare at him hard, searching for clues. They don't know if he's lying or not, but there's no denying that his proposal, if legitimate, will interest Ice. He has been talking a lot lately about focusing less on war, more on making money—which isn't to say he isn't as suspicious of the Crips' intentions as Steed and the rest of his surviving soldiers are.

When word first came down that Tony wanted to set up a meeting, Ice immediately thought it was a ploy to bring him out into the open. But Ice also knew he had nothing to lose by sending a delegation to talk with Tony. J-Roc would scope it out beforehand and only green-light the meeting if he were sure it wasn't a trap. As long as Tony was on his own, there was no risk in hearing him out. Steed could pop him if he needed to and, depending on what he said, might pop him even if he didn't need to.

But now, Tony's talking like the Crips really *do* want to quash the beef. He's lamenting how "out of hand" things have gotten, telling them that when an "innocent girl" like Leticia gets caught up in hostilities, and a "good kid" like Doc gets murdered, it means things have gone too far.

"For real, we don't need this shit no more," Tony says. "We ain't never going to be aight with you all grinding in our hood, but we could at least take shit back to the way it was before, when there weren't all these bodies getting dropped."

"You talking about a truce?" Steed asks.

"Call it what you want," says Tony. "What I'm talking about is, no more shooting, no more beefing like we been. Way Tyrek sees it, we both making money in the territory we got. We'll be making even more if we chill with the beef and don't give the cops more reasons to be up in our shit."

Tony and Steed agree to take all details of the meeting back to their respective gang leaders. Phone numbers are exchanged, so that the crews can set up a summit and potentially hash out a truce.

❧

"They bite?" Tyrek asks Tony in the Crips clubhouse afterward.

"They done bit all the way," Tony says.

A meeting between Tyrek and Ice, along with each man's lieutenants, is scheduled for three days later. As a show of good faith, both sides agree not to carry out any attacks in the interim. The detente holds, and when the eve of the meeting arrives, there's real optimism on the part of the Bloods that the war's end is at hand.

The Crips play the part of battle-fatigued soldiers ready to lay down their arms. Their plan going forward is simple: Wait until Ice and his lieutenants pull up at the designated meeting spot, then unleash a fusillade of gunfire on their vehicle.

Laying in wait will be two Crips gunmen, stationed inside an abandoned house and ready to open fire from behind the home's already-broken windows.

"We fittin' to make real moves on them slobs now," Tyrek says.

"They ain't got no chance," says Tony. "You too smart for them niggas, yo."

The men spark up a blunt and smoke it while Tony drives them to Rock's new house. The Crips hitter recently rented a mansion on Nassau's North Shore, where his is "the only black face for miles, other than the nannies and the drivers," he says. Tonight, his bosses are coming over to finalize details of what Tyrek's taken to calling their Trojan Horse mission—and to celebrate their impending victory.

Turning off of Linden Place, they head up Peninsula and pass the building where Tyrek once lived two floors down from Patrice Cunningham. He still thinks about her sometimes, wonders where she ended up, how her life turned out. He'd always wanted to tell her he was sorry for stabbing her, even though it was all that dumb-ass Steed's fault for jumping out that way like a bitch instead of stepping up and fighting, he thinks.

Even now, with all the women Tyrek has around, he'd still rather have Patrice. The girl was fine, and she sweated him, too, Tyrek thinks, always flirting with him even though she swore she was Steed's girl. They'd have ended up together, he believes, if that fool hadn't messed everything up. With Patrice on his arm, maybe things would have turned out different. Maybe he'd have gone legit and gotten rich outside the game, freeing him from dealing with these Bloods clowns—and the fear of his own assassination—every day.

But there's no use dwelling on the past, he knows. If he wants to stay on top and remain "king" of Hempstead's underworld—as he likes to think of himself—he must focus relentlessly on the present. For Steed will no doubt seek revenge soon for that bloody afternoon six years earlier.

In Tyrek's view, there's no chance that "coward" will avenge Patrice's stabbing. For that day had showed him everything he needed to know about the two of them: One was strong, the other, weak. One stayed the course, the other escaped to LA. And when this war is over, he says, "only one going to still be breathing."

As they head toward Rock's house, Tony and Tyrek take in the sights, watching the world around them transform. In these overwhelmingly white, low-crime suburbs, even the neighborhood names sound nicer: Garden City, Mineola, Roslyn, Westbury, Syosset, Oyster Bay. The houses are newer and prettier than those in Hempstead, their lawns well kept, their streets nearly spotless. The storefront windows dazzle with expensive merchandise. The smell of delicious food wafts from one classy restaurant after another.

Out here, most people are blissfully unaware of the violence perpetrated in places like Hempstead, Freeport, and Roosevelt, clueless to the extent of their poverty, failing schools, and traumatized children. In these tony neighborhoods, the comfort and well-being of Long Islanders *depends* on them not thinking about it. When folks out here learn about drug and gang shootings on the news or read about them in the paper, they wonder what the Island is coming to, then change the channel or turn the page.

"As long as they keep all that violence in their own neighborhoods, I say leave them be," says Rosemary Smith, a high school teacher from Garden City. "They're going to kill each other no matter where you put them—the city, Long Island, anywhere. Just keep it off my block and away from my kids. They do that? I say 'Live and let live.'"

Her husband, Ronald, a Nassau County government official, has a different view.

"I say carpet-bomb Hempstead and start over, because it's never going to be a safe, livable place," Ronald says. "It will never be the kind of community where your average New Yorker will feel comfortable raising a family. It's a slum. With a place like that, you kind of just have to tear it all down and start from scratch. Let the blacks and Hispanics go back to New York City. They're better off there. Long Island isn't that kind of place."

Just about the only time gang violence encroaches on the lives of the Smiths and their neighbors is when some addict or corner boy gets gunned down or stabbed inside the Garden City or Mineola border, in which case their death might rate a news story. When that happens, the Smiths and their neighbors pay attention for a little while. They ponder the ugliness of those lives being lived just a few blocks away, but just as quickly, they forget.

"It's just a shame you can't drive through some of those neighborhoods [in Hempstead] anymore," says Rosemary. "Because there are still some really beautiful spots."

"We even thought about buying a Mercedes until we realized where the service center was," Ronald says.

Tyrek and Tony pass the Smiths' two-story Colonial on their way to Rock's house. Closer to the shore, they see opulent, multimillion-dollar mansions with tall steel gates and backyards big as football fields. Kids play soccer and hockey in the street. Mothers push around strollers that cost more than most of the cars lining Linden Place.

"I'll take all this," Tony says. "I'd trade places with any of them."

"Nigga, we done come a long way," Tyrek says. "We done did shit these people ain't never have the heart for. If they were born in our shoes, they'd be dead already."

"Word," Tony says, nodding. "You right. We getting paid."

"There you go," Tyrek says. "And pretty soon, you might have as much as these white folks. If things go the way I plan."

When they reach Rock's place, they hear hip-hop blaring from the backyard. They knock and are greeted by a Crips hooker, one of several

Rock chauffeured out here for the party. Inside, the Big Homies take turns with the women in between pulling on blunts and sucking down Coronas and Hennessy. Rock shows off some of his new toys: a gold-plated AK-47, an American military-issued hand grenade, and a diamond-encrusted silencer.

"So your soldiers are ready for tomorrow?" Tyrek says.

"For sure, my nigga," Rock says. "They tooled up. They professionals. Ain't going to be no problems."

"Good," says Tyrek. "Then we almost finished with these niggas."

Back in Hempstead, alone in his apartment, Ice contemplates Tyrek's peace proposal. Is it a trick, or the way out of the gang war he has been hoping for? He doesn't have the will to continue fighting the Crips, he knows. After nearly a year of battle, he's tired of the endless retaliatory violence and threat of arrest, sick of constantly watching his back for fear he'll be scooped up by the cops or murdered by his enemies. His flashbacks are growing more frequent, his nightmares more intense. If he doesn't get out of the game soon, he says, he'll either die, get locked up again, or go insane.

For a long time now, he has gotten by on his roughneck front—a well-honed, hard-case pose that never betrays a hint of self-doubt or insecurity. But it's getting tougher to keep it up.

"Only the strong survive in this game," he says. "And there was a time, no doubt, when I was the craziest nigga out here. I mixed business knowledge with street knowledge and made myself a whole lot of money. Got more than a mil saved up, in fact. I even helped some niggas get educated, schooled them on history, finance, anything they was interested in. I felt like I had a purpose. But if I'm being honest? Now? I ain't got the strength to keep this shit going. If you going to be in the game, you've got to be in all the way. No such thing as being halfway in this. Halfway gets you killed or gets you caught."

He picks up a burner and dials his aunt Cheryl's number. He should take her up on her offer, he thinks—leave for Atlanta and start his own accounting firm. But before Cheryl can answer, Ice ends the call, seeing the fault in his logic. He can't just quit now, he thinks, not after he'd spent years building a lucrative drug business in his hometown that earns him about $700,000 a year after payroll and expenses. How else can he make that kind of money, with felonies on his record and no post-prison employment history?

"Even if I had a profitable little accounting business down there, I'd never come close to what I make up here," he says.

Then there's the matter of his men. What would become of all the young hustlers who depend on him for their livelihood? If Ice walks away, he knows, they'll be ostracized for having shown loyalty to such a cowardly boss. Their reputations in the game will be ruined, with the Crips running them out of town—or worse.

"What they going to do for work if I run off?" he says.

Ice is torn between what he considers the two distinct halves of his personality: the businessman and the gangster. The businessman is rational, intelligent, and aware that he's playing a losing game against his competitors. The gangster is prideful and stubborn, refusing to bow to his enemies.

On this day, the gangster wins out. Ice decides to stay, to take a gamble on the peace offer. If it's legitimate, he says, he'll accept it. If it's not, he'll keep fighting.

"If Tyrek's going to take me out, he's going to have to outwit me," he says. "And if that nigga outwits me, I don't deserve to be king nohow."

CHAPTER FOURTEEN

In Country

In terms of human capital, they have so much . . . it's impossible to stop the dealing.

—Detective Delahunt

"What we need," Reverend Lyons tells his audience, "is to get through to these young men before another tragedy occurs." Lyons has gathered a large crowd of black clergy, antiviolence activists, ex-gang members, and concerned residents from around Hempstead for a gang-outreach event he has been touting for weeks. He made sure all the local Bloods and Crips received fliers for the event. His marchers even pleaded with the crews in person to stop by for the loads of free soul food.

But when it's time to begin, there's not a single active gang member in the church hall. The only person who appears part of the target audience is a high, forlorn-looking junkie who stumbles his way through the buffet line, fills his plate with food, and nods off in the back of the hall.

Meanwhile, the clergymen give speeches geared toward a thug audience that never shows up. "I was like you all," says Richard Weatherspoon, a former Crip who'd served a long prison term and now speaks to at-risk youth about the dangers of gang life. "I was after that money, running with guns and selling drugs. But I turned my life around. It's not easy, but if you decide to change, it can be done."

"Tell it!" the audience responds.

The anti-violence activists seen marching here employ a novel strategy: midnight prayer walks in which they roam the village's war-torn drug markets, looking for gang members and addicts with whom to pray. Many of the marchers are former junkies or gang members themselves, having once sowed mayhem on the same streets they now find themselves trying to clean up.
STEVE PFOST

But the speakers are quite literally preaching to the choir. All the men and women in the hall are churchgoing folks who have already lifted themselves out of the drug culture, raised families, and escaped the grip of addiction and violence. The clergymen give inspirational speeches about salvaging the community, and the activists speak movingly of never giving up on Hempstead's youth. But when the event ends, it's unclear whether any real impact has been made, for the gangsters they'd hoped to reach are on their corners instead of here. Even the junkie who wandered in seems to understand the evening's been a letdown.

"Those were some good speeches," he tells one of the pastors as he stumbles out of the church. "But you all need to get some corner boys in here next time."

Still, the night was not a waste, for one corner boy had indeed gotten the message. Passing by outside the church earlier that night, Devon LaFleur had heard Lyons's booming voice and—unbeknownst to those inside—stopped to listen to a few cautionary tales about the gang war swallowing his neighborhood.

The clergymen's messages drove home the truth of Devon's situation: If he didn't find a way out of the Bloods soon, he'd likely meet the same grim fate as an increasing number of his corner colleagues.

"This ain't me," he tells his mother when he gets home. "I want to get out of it, but there ain't no way to."

"What do you mean, there's no way?" Toni LaFleur says. "You just walk away. Don't let those fools drag you down with them."

Leaving the Bloods isn't like quitting a job, Devon tells her. In this game, there's no quitting. Once a Blood, he says, you're a Blood for life.

"I'd have to get on a plane and go to, like, Alaska or something. I'd have to leave here and not come back, because they wouldn't let me be."

He makes a slashing motion across his throat to demonstrate what would happen if he were to tell the crew he's quitting.

"For real, Devon?" Toni asks.

"Hells yeah," he says. "They don't play. I knew that going in, though."

"Only one thing left to do then," Toni says. "I'm going to save up enough to put you on a plane. You going go stay with your aunt Jasmine in South Carolina until we figure out what comes next."

"Carolina? Ain't nothing down there for me."

"You got a better plan? Because as far as I can tell, you all out of options. Running your only one."

Devon clicks his tongue in disapproval, staring out the kitchen window at fellow Bloods serving drive-up customers on MLK. The corners are busy tonight. Lots of money to be made, he thinks.

"It ain't fair," Devon says. "Why do people got to get killed behind making their living? Why can't it just be a job, something you do without all the drama behind it?"

Toni doesn't offer an answer. Instead, she finds a notebook and pencil and starts adding up expenses—plane ticket, dining costs, cab fare—to calculate how much she'll need to send her son down south.

"I'm not going to let them hurt you," she says.

Devon laughs, kisses his mother on the cheek, and heads for the door. He's working the overnight shift tonight and, barring a police sweep, will be standing on his designated drug corner—rain or shine—for the next six hours.

"Love you, Ma," he says before leaving. "But you ain't hearing me. No way out this game."

Detective Delahunt is driving through the neighborhood about three hours later, still hunting for leads in the spate of recent gang murders, when Devon sees his car turn down MLK.

"Five-o! Five-o!" he shouts. The Bloods dealing crew, along with half a dozen pipeheads they've attracted, drop whatever incriminating items they're holding and try to act natural. Delahunt rolls his eyes at the half-hearted display. He's been playing this game with the Crips and Bloods crews all year—he'll drive by, and they'll shut down the Shop until he clears the block. Sometimes, he'll jump out and make a bust, maybe nail a corner boy or two on a possession charge to try and flip them. But no matter how many he brings in, there's always someone there to replace them.

"In terms of human capital, they have so much . . . it's impossible to stop the dealing," Delahunt says, inching his car up beside Devon. "The brass [in the police department] knows that's the case, too. Unless you put a charge on every kid in the neighborhood, simultaneously, someone's going to be ready to work the stash. For them, the money outweighs the risks."

Delahunt lowers his window, asking Devon why he's on the corner at two a.m. instead of in bed.

"How you supposed to get up for school when you're out here doing dirt?" the detective asks.

Devon knows Delahunt from the neighborhood basketball courts, where the cop sometimes stops by for games once his shift ends. Devon likes him, too, but knows there will be hell to pay if Ice or Steed sees him talking all friendly with a five-o. They'd already given him shit for chatting with Mike Clary a few months back.

"Yo, you going to get me in trouble," Devon says, before realizing he could be in trouble with Delahunt, too. "You ain't locking me up, are you?"

"Not unless you're holding," he says.

"I ain't," Devon says. "You could search me, even."

"I'm giving you a warning is all," Delahunt says. "But I come back and see you standing here later? I'm going to have to start rounding your people up."

"Yes, sir."

"Go home, D-Bo. Stop messing with these fools."

Back at police headquarters, Delahunt wonders how long it will be before Devon catches a bullet.

"The kid's not built for this," he says. "The hard part is helping them find out what they *are* built for. That takes time, though. And they want money now."

With Delahunt gone, Devon goes inside the Bloods clubhouse to tell Steed about his warning.

"He says if he sees me out there when he comes back, he's going to round our people up."

Steed checks his watch, does a little math in his head. Ice has long set daily profit quotas for his crews, and Steed risks coming up short if the Shop doesn't stay open overnight. At the same time, Steed knows having his best corner supervisor locked up would lead to even more losses.

"Aight, we going to shut down for a couple hours until this stupid-ass cop off the clock," Steed says. "You come back at ten a.m. We'll open the Shop then."

"Okay. I can get paid now, though, right?" Devon says, remembering his mom's South Carolina plan.

"Nigga, you ain't even worked a full shift," Steed says. "You'll get paid tomorrow when you finish."

"But yo, I need that money."

"Nigga, did I stutter? Get up outta here. Don't make me tell you again."

So Devon goes home, where his mother's still sitting at the kitchen table crunching numbers to figure out how to send him down south. She fixes him some Hamburger Helper, tells him everything's going to be fine.

"This time next year," she says, "you'll be living in the country, safe and sound. New school, new everything. And as soon as I save up enough, I'm going to move out there with you. We'll get our own place."

"Shoot, you know we broke, Ma," he says, ruing the fact that he'd blown nearly all his corner money on clothes, jewelry, and expensive dates. He'd need at least two weeks of wages to be able to comfortably afford the move, plus expenses he'd accrue down south looking for a new job.

With a war raging, two weeks seemed a long way off.

"I ain't even get paid tonight. Can't afford to move nowhere."

"Let me worry about the money," she says. "In the meantime, you just keep away from them Crips."

Devon says he wishes he could steer clear of the enemy crew, but he knows they'll be coming back with their guns soon. They always do.

"Ain't no way outta this," he says, walking off to his bedroom for some shut-eye before his shift resumes. "That's why the game's the game."

After work the next day, Devon thinks about riding his bike over to the mall like he did most weekends before joining the Bloods. Or maybe he'll head to the arcade. But he quickly realizes both places are off limits to him now, falling within the boundaries of different crews—one linked to the notoriously violent gang MS-13, Mara Salvatrucha, and the other, to a Guatemalan organization known for selling strong Mexican heroin.

When his friend Lionel calls him up and invites him over to watch basketball on his family's new flat-screen, Devon says he can't. The trip to Lionel's—a fifteen-minute ride he used to make on his bike two or three times a week—would take him through the territory of other enemy crews, including the Crips.

"Why can't you just ride through real fast?" Lionel says, unable to comprehend how something like a gang's turf lines could keep him from seeing his friend. "What if you just keep your head down and don't look at any of them boys? Then they'll just let you ride on through, won't they?"

"It ain't like that," Devon says. "I mean, some of those crews *might* let me pass. But they might not. Depends on how they're feeling at that moment . . . maybe who else they're beefing with, whether they've been dealing with other drama. But I'd just be riding in blind, taking a big-ass risk."

"Damn," Lionel says. "What about your moms? Can't she drive you here? I could ask my dad to give you a ride back later on. He'd be aight with that."

"Nah, my moms ain't going to be home until late. She working a double today."

There's a long silence between them then, as if both boys are just realizing the impossibility of their friendship amid these new conditions.

"This crazy, yo," Lionel says. "How we going to chill again if you can't ride through no neighborhood but your own? I mean, how you supposed to go *anywhere* without crossing through some other crew's territory?"

"I don't know, yo. I'm trying to figure that out myself. Can't see no way."

"Damn," Lionel says.

"I know," says Devon.

Lionel calls Devon a few more times over the next few weeks to invite him over, once even urging him to come camping with his family in Westchester County, north of New York City. But Devon's afraid to travel so far from home without any of his crew. What if he ran into some upstate Crips and they stepped to him? He couldn't throw down in front of Lionel's parents, but if he punked out in a fight, word would surely get back to Ice and Steed; his gangland reputation, which he'd worked so hard to cultivate these past few months, would instantly be ruined.

So he says no to the camping trip, as well as the other invitations his friend makes. Steadily, their phone chats become less frequent, until there are none at all.

Just up the street from Devon's house, Bolo Jay and Rock sit in an SUV, Bolo rapping the lyrics to "Rapper's Delight" to keep himself occupied. They've been watching Devon for days now, studying what time he leaves home, what time he returns, and where he goes in between. It's part of their current mission, which involves learning the movements and specific duties of all Bloods leaders and supervisors. Their goal is to map every aspect of the gang's drug-distribution operation and, armed with that information, to destroy Ice's set through shootings, stash-house robberies, and anything else Tyrek deems necessary—including the Trojan Horse mission Rock's been plotting these past few weeks.

"Nigga, quit rapping a minute and let me school you up," Rock says. "Don't you want to learn how this shit's done?"

Bolo quits mid-verse and tells Rock he's ready to "get schooled."

"Aight, let me ask you: Do you know why we doing so much surveillance last few days?" Rock asks. "You know why we watching these niggas like hawks at they cribs and on they corners?"

"Why?" Bolo says.

"Because if you know your enemy better than he knows himself," Rock says, "then you going beat him, no matter what. Always remember that. Knowledge of the opposition is everything in this here game. Just like in business. Just like in war."

Since their murder of Lamar, Rock's become a kind of mentor to Bolo, teaching him the ins and outs of the drug game and schooling him on the best ways to find, follow, and kill a target. Bolo looks up to Rock, viewing him as an older-brother figure who rescued him from Tyrek and Tony's doghouse. As Bolo sees it, Rock plucked him from obscurity to become his sidekick and hitter-in-training—one of the top positions in the gang. Bolo now views his bosses in an almost saintly light, believing they're the models by which all other hustlers in the neighborhood should be measured.

Bolo, when quizzed, doesn't know the name of the vice president of the United States or New York's governor, or which county he lives in; he can't even read beyond a first-grade level. But he knows Tyrek and Tony's complete biographies, knows they're the leaders of his set and the smartest, toughest gangsters in New York. In his world, they're more worthy of adulation than a vice president or governor could ever be. Luminaries outside the Triangle, he knows, have no bearing on life here.

"You just keep your eyes and ears open, just keep learning and stay hungry, and you'll rise quick," Rock says as they watch Devon's house. "If you stay on point, Tyrek going to do right by you."

Bolo nods, then takes the bump of coke Rock offers him. They've been using more of the stuff lately during downtime on their missions. As long as they don't do too much, Rock says, there's no harm in it.

"We only using this shit on stakeouts," Rock declares after taking his own sniff. "It's good for staying awake when you got to watch somebody. But don't make a habit of it. Tyrek don't like nobody working for him to use his product. This a special case, though."

"Aight," Bolo says. "Makes sense."

Bolo's only done coke during their stakeouts, but he has enjoyed it every time. He sometimes brings a few bags home to his foster mom, Alicia, who became his and Alex's legal guardian after his real mom overdosed. Alicia prefers rocks to powder, and since crack is the gang's specialty, he's able to keep her supplied with more of the stuff than she can use. In return, she doesn't hassle Bolo about not going to school. As long as he gets her those rocks, she's happy.

Life's pretty good, he thinks. Better than it ever was when he was sitting in class every day. Now he's got a reputation, respect, and more than enough money to keep Alex decked out in nice clothes for school.

Still, this mission involving D-Bo makes him a little queasy, since they'd once been friends. Devon tutored him in math for hours when he had trouble keeping up in class. And when Devon's mom packed an extra snack into his lunch, Devon always gave it to Bolo, since he never had any money before going to work for the Crips.

Now, just because Devon's joined a rival gang, Bolo's being forced to do something that will probably end up hurting his old friend. Maybe he and Rock would be ordered to shoot Devon. Or maybe they'd have to stick him up one day and steal his crew's package and profits. Either way, he knows, Devon will end up broke, defeated, and maybe dead, since that's what Tyrek has planned for all the Hempstead Bloods.

After a few more bumps, Bolo tells Rock about his relationship with Devon, figuring it might earn the Bloods member a reprieve.

"Nigga, don't you ever talk about one of these slobs being your friend," Rock says. "He wasn't never your friend. He's the mothafucking enemy, you feel me?"

"Yeah, my bad," Bolo says.

They sit in silence watching Devon's house until he comes out at six p.m., just like he does every night. They follow him as he walks to a Bloods corner off MLK, greets his crew, and starts serving customers.

He looks the same as he did in math class, Bolo thinks, the same as he did when they were friends. Now, though, he has to hate the kid. And he will. If Rock, Tyrek, and Tony say Devon's the enemy, then it must be true.

CHAPTER FIFTEEN

Kings

Time to earn your pay.

—Tyrek

The day of the Trojan Horse ambush, two Crips soldiers selected for the mission—Flex Butler and Savant Sharpe—arrive early at the abandoned house in order to prepare. It's a habit they picked up from Rock, who's known to get to jobs three or four hours ahead of time to ensure "no one gets the drop" on him.

"In this game, if you want to be successful, you got to show up way ahead of time for your missions," says Rock. "Because if the people you're coming after show up first . . . if they better prepared than you? Shit, that's going to be all she wrote for your late ass."

Ice, still suspicious of Tyrek's intentions, sends J-Roc to scout out the meeting spot. His sole job is to make sure the peace summit isn't a trap, but having gotten high on his own weed supply beforehand, J-Roc fails to search the house occupied by Savant and Flex. Seeing nothing suspicious, he calls Ice and gives the all clear.

"We on," Ice tells Steed and Super Curt, his newly promoted second lieutenant, as they pile into Steed's Yukon and head for the summit. Each is armed and on alert for any sign of trouble. But having been assured by their advance man that nothing's out of place, they're feeling more relaxed.

"We going to be all good," Ice assures them.

A few minutes later, Flex sees Steed's Yukon approaching and calls Rock to alert him. Rock, who's parked in a Beamer on the next block, starts for the house, too. The Crips gunmen perched at the window make one last check of their semiautomatic weapons. Finally, the Yukon comes to a stop halfway up the block.

"This the spot," says Steed. The Beamer rolls up from the opposite direction a few seconds later. "Looks like everyone's here," Ice says, exiting the Yukon along with his lieutenants. "Let's do this."

The driver's-side door of the Beamer swings open, the Crips watching closely to see who'll step out. Ice thinks he can glimpse Rock behind the heavily tinted windshield. But as quickly as it opened, the door slams shut. It's the signal Savant and Flex have been waiting for. They tear the window curtain away, raise their semiautos, and unleash a hail of gunfire at the three Bloods. The first shots strike the side of the Yukon, tearing holes in its doors and shattering its windows. The metallic clinks of lead slashing through metal echo through the neighborhood.

Then, the bullets begin to find their targets. Steed is the first one hit, struck in his lower back as he runs toward the Yukon's passenger-side door. He collapses in the street as two more slugs tear into his legs. Super Curt is the next to fall. One round blows a piece of flesh off his arm and a second rips through his shoulder. He stumbles to the pavement and crawls around to the rear of the Yukon. There, a third bullet pierces his neck, and he goes still.

Ice, having hit the ground when the first shot rang out, manages to crawl around to the other side of the SUV, using it as a shield. He grabs Steed's arm and drags him to cover. "At least two niggas shooting," Ice says. "Let's bang out, yo. Empty that clip."

They both pull nine-millimeters from their waistbands and return fire toward the window, ducking out from behind the Yukon long enough to get off a few rounds, then returning to cover. They repeat this several times before the muzzle flashes in the window cease.

"They hit?" Steed asks.

"Don't know," says Ice.

They wait behind the Yukon, breathing hard, the street quiet now except for a distant car alarm. Then they hear it: the patter of sneakers on grass, then on pavement, followed by a screech of rubber. The Beamer pulls up in front of the house as Flex and Savant come sprinting out, guns raised and ready to fire should Ice or Steed peek their heads out again. The pair jump in the Beamer and Rock speeds off.

Ice runs out to the middle of the street and takes aim at the back of the getaway car, but it's already too far gone. He slides the nine back into his waistband, runs over to Steed, and helps him to his feet.

"We got to move fast," he says.

Steed's jeans are soaked with blood, as is his lower back. He's having trouble keeping his eyes open, and Ice knows he must get his lieutenant to a doctor quickly or risk him bleeding out. He slings Steed's arm around his neck and half drags, half carries him toward an old, unlocked Camry parked nearby. Ice quickly hot-wires the car and peels out, Steed stretched across the backseat. He races back toward Hempstead, hauls his wounded friend out of the car, and drags him up Graham Avenue.

"Keep your eyes open," Ice says. "Take even breaths, yo."

They make it to the porch of a bungalow-style home and Ice pounds on the door, holding Steed up with his other arm. There's no answer for one minute, then two.

Finally, when Marsha Ricks can no longer ignore the banging, when she's convinced herself the boy out there bleeding deserves to live no matter what he's done or who he's done it to, she opens up.

"Thank you, Mrs. Ricks," Ice says. He has known her since he was a little kid, knows her reputation as a kind, patient woman. She'd once told him to come to her if he ever wanted to get out of gang life and needed help starting fresh. And as a friend of his aunt Cheryl's, Ricks was just as fierce a proponent of him moving to Atlanta as she was.

"Can you help him?" Ice says. "I thought maybe your son could do something."

"Get him inside," Ricks says. "Lord have mercy."

Right away she calls her son, William, a medical student doing his residency in New Jersey, and begs him to come help.

He refuses at first, telling her to call for an ambulance and get Steed to a hospital before it's too late. She explains what Ice had told her: that a trip to the emergency room for multiple gunshot wounds would attract the attention of police. Since Steed had outstanding warrants for missing court in a handful of drug cases, he'd surely end up back behind bars after being treated.

William Ricks still declines to help, scolding his mother for "harboring two criminals." Then she starts in about how William himself ran with gangsters when he was a kid in the neighborhood and only escaped their fate because of his parents' tough love. After ten minutes of intense back-and-forth, with his mother playing every card she has, William relents.

"I'll do this one time, Mom," he says. "But you've got to stop acting like the ghetto Mother Teresa. And you've got to seriously think about moving out here, okay?"

"Okay, sweetheart," Marsha Ricks says. "Just hurry."

William arrives an hour later carrying two satchels full of medical supplies, which he uses to clean and dress Steed's wounds after stemming the bleeding. Against all odds, the Crips lieutenant appears to stabilize.

"You ought to play the lotto," William says. "A few inches one way or another on this back wound, we wouldn't be talking right now."

"So he's going to be aight?" Ice says.

"I just mean he's lucky he's not dead," says William. "But what we're doing here is only going to buy him a little time. He needs to get to a hospital within the next day, or we're looking at a serious possibility of infection and any number of other potential issues that could be life-threatening."

"I can't go to no hospital," Steed says. "Police going to be looking in all the ERs after what went down."

"So, you'd rather risk your life than go to jail?" asks William.

"Jail? Psshh. More like prison, yo. Judge suspended my sentence as long as I stayed out of trouble and made my court dates. But I missed some, so I'd probably be looking at the full sentence. Five years."

"Listen to me closely," William says. "You could die. Is that clear to you?"

"Yeah, I know," Steed says. "But this how it's got to play."

"You could drive him to an ER somewhere in Jersey," Ricks tells her son. "I'd imagine the police here wouldn't be looking in hospitals out there."

William looks at his mom, shakes his head.

"You're unbelievable," he says. But he can't risk letting this kid die. William and Steed set off for a Jersey hospital. Ice stays behind to plot the Bloods' retaliation and get with Super Curt's family about planning his funeral.

"We got more heart than them Crips niggas any day," Steed says before they part ways. "Don't let them win, yo."

"No doubt," Ice says, hugging his last surviving lieutenant. "You let me know where you're at, and I'll be up when things quiet down."

Then it's just Ice and Marsha Ricks alone in her home, an old church-going woman raised in the segregated South and a young drug dealer who rules half the territory outside her door. They watch an episode of *Judge Judy* and she fixes him a plate of her best chicken and potatoes, while trying to talk him out of returning to the corners. After dinner he tells her he has to go; there's business he must attend to.

"I know what business that is, Michael," she says. "That business nearly got you and your friend killed. Why don't you stay here until things calm down? I've got plenty of room. And you seem to like the cooking."

"I appreciate it, Mrs. Ricks, but I've got responsibilities," Ice says.

"You got to go back to selling drugs, you mean."

"Ma'am, with all due respect, staying here ain't going to help me deal with what's waiting out there. That world's going to be there tomorrow, be there a week from now, and a year from now. The longer I wait to go back, the harder it gets for me to keep doing what I do."

"I just don't want you to get shot. Neither does your aunt," Ricks says. "I know what's going on out there. I hear it outside my windows every night. You and your friend got lucky, that's all. Ain't that you survived because you're tougher—it's just dumb luck. You want to keep relying on luck to keep you alive?"

"You right, there's some luck in the game. But you got to have more than that."

He points to his head, then to his heart.

Ricks waves a hand in dismissal. "You can't outthink a bullet, because it don't have nobody's name on it," she says. "You can't out-tough a bullet, neither. We just want you to make it out of here alive."

"Bye, Mrs. Ricks."

In a moment, he's limping down the street, his practiced roughneck front switched back on. He retrieves one of his cars, a Lexus, and drives to a Bloods safe house in Riverhead, sixty miles east of Hempstead.

Still got a chance to beat these niggas, he thinks.

———

Later, when Tyrek hears Ice and Steed survived the ambush, he's livid.

"How'd those niggas miss?" Tyrek asks. "Got-damn."

"Flex and Savant carried that shit," Rock says. "Those two bitches just got lucky."

"Aight, but it's a fucking mess we got here."

"I'll clean it up."

"You best," says Tyrek. "Time to earn your pay."

Rock patrols Hempstead all night in search of Ice and Steed. He stops at every store in town to ask if anyone's seen them, checks in with every Crips informant. But there's no sign of the Bloods leaders.

"I'm thinking maybe they left town," Rock says when Tyrek calls him for an update. "Ain't nobody spotted them."

Tyrek's yelling into the phone, cursing the Bloods, when Rock interrupts him.

"Got-damn, there go that mothafucka's whip right there!"

Rock hangs up and chases after a passing Lexus like the one Ice drives. It stops at a red light, giving him time to catch up. He reaches into the glove box for his Luger, steps out of his car, and walks up to the Lexus's half-opened driver's-side window.

"No!" a woman screams.

Rock sees it's not Ice in the car, but only a large, scared-looking lady in a nurse's uniform and her two little girls seated in the back, neither older than four or five. The children begin to cry when they see the gun pointed at their mother.

"My bad," Rock says.

"Please don't kill me."

"Get up outta here," he says, lowering the Luger and walking back to his car.

The woman speeds off and calls the cops, but Rock's long gone by the time they arrive.

"Wasn't them," he tells Tyrek back at the clubhouse.

"Nigga, you on my last nerve," Tyrek says. "I feel like we playing *Where's Waldo* and shit. Where them bitch niggas at?"

———

Ice spends several days hiding out at his Riverhead safe house, maintaining regular contact with the remainder of his crew, telling them to stay off their corners and out of sight. They must keep low profiles, he says, because cops are out in force following the shoot-out that killed Super Curt. Rock's almost certainly hunting for them, too.

Ice is far from the action, but he keeps in touch. A day after the shoot-out, the wounded Steed called to say he was in a hospital and feeling much better. They'd performed surgery to remove a bullet and were keeping him loaded up on painkillers.

"This stuff better than weed, yo," said Steed. "*This* the shit we should be selling."

Ice laughed at his lieutenant, told him to heal up and wait for his word.

"We'll be back up in no time," Ice said.

But the truth is, he's worried. Every day his crew is off the corners, they're losing money as well as respect. Their crack and weed supplies sit untouched in various stash houses throughout the neighborhood, all drug deliveries and sales suspended, all orders put on hold. It's a lull like this all dealers fear, because ceasing operations in one's territory—even for a few days—tends to embolden other crews looking to claim vacant corners.

Empty streets on a gang's turf are a sign of weakness—and often precede defeat.

"Maybe Tyrek decides to put his people down there, claim MLK as his own. Claim victory and shit."

That's the scenario Ice is hoping to avoid when, following a fifth straight day off the corners in mid-November, he orders J-Roc, Big Boy Owens, and a few junior Bloods to return to MLK with a small package of crack. They're all the soldiers he has left aside from D-Bo, his top corner supervisor, who isn't answering his calls.

"Smart kid," Ice says of Devon. "He wants to live. Boy was always too smart for this here game."

Ice, resigned to working with this depleted crew, lays out some basic instructions to J-Roc and Big Boy: Move their g-pack while gathering intelligence on any new competitors, police presence, and Crips patrols. Then, call him with an update.

"We on it," J-Roc says.

At first, all appears to be just as the Bloods had left it. Old customers who had ventured to the Triangle for the past week and been disappointed begin returning to the MLK market as word spreads of its reopening.

By late afternoon, the g-pack is nearly sold out. J-Roc calls Ice to ask if they should re-up.

"What you seeing out there?" Ice asks.

"All good so far," says J-Roc. "Police be staring us down and shit when they roll past but ain't none jumped out. Ain't no detectives come down asking about no shootings, either. Crips is steady slinging in the Triangle, but they ain't been down here but to patrol like regular."

"They ain't made a play for our corners?"

"Not from what I'm hearing," J-Roc says. "I asked around, and everyone say MLK been a ghost town. No other crews been down here. Crips was just letting our customers come to them, seems like."

"Aight, keep it going," Ice says. "But you best not be wrong about this the way you was with that meeting."

J-Roc quickly orders the re-up from a nearby stash apartment. In the same project building, Flex Butler, disguised in what he calls his "hood rat costume"—consisting of a blonde wig and Gucci women's sunglasses—pretends to talk on his cell phone. He watches Big Boy walk out of the stash apartment carrying a backpack filled with crack vials. A few minutes later, the backpack's in the hands of J-Roc and the rest of his corner crew, its contents already being traded to pipeheads for bills.

Flex, watching all this from an upstairs window, dials Rock's burner.

"They just moved the re-up," Flex says. "Nobody even guarding the stash spot."

"Good job, yo," says Rock.

Two minutes later, he pulls up behind the projects, his car full of heavily armed Crips, including Bolo. Flex hurries downstairs and opens the rear emergency door for Rock and his men. He loses the wig and glasses and joins the crew of soldiers as they race up to the third floor, gathering outside the Bloods' stash apartment. Rock gives them a countdown and they burst in through the unlocked door. The three kids inside—twelve- and thirteen-year-old Bloods associates—look stunned.

"Don't even think about it, nigga," Rock says when one kid makes a move toward his waist.

Bolo tosses three empty duffel bags onto the floor and orders the kids to pack them up with their stash. They do as they're told, retrieving all the coke in the closet, about $20,000 worth, and stuffing it inside the bags.

"Tell Ice his stashes going to keep getting took until he shows his face like a man," says Rock. "Tell him Tyrek says he a punk-ass bitch, and he ain't got the heart for this here war. He either crawl out from wherever he hiding his bitch ass, or we take down his packages, his money, and his crew till he do. Tell him they only one king around here, and he ain't it."

Rock and his men leave with the stolen crack and bring it down to the Triangle, where it's sold alongside their own product. Customers who'd been returning to MLK now hurry to the Triangle for their rush-hour fix. Meanwhile, the surviving Bloods soldiers pace their empty corners, furious and ashamed.

"We looking like dummies right now, for real," J-Roc says.

He calls Ice to report the robbery, relaying Rock's message verbatim.

"Tyrek called you out, straight up, yo. Called you a bitch."

Ice retrieves a bulletproof vest from his closet, steels himself with a swig of Hennessy, and grabs his car keys.

But on his way out the door, something gives him pause. He goes back inside and calls his aunt, tells her he loves her, asks her to pray for his soul should he fall. He might not see her again, he says.

"I love you, Auntie."

She begs him not to return to Hempstead, tells him that whatever static he's involved in isn't worth his life.

"They called me out," Ice says. "I've got to answer."

"Don't go, Michael," she says.

"I love you," Ice repeats, hanging up before she can say it back.

<hr />

Ice covers the sixty miles to Hempstead in less than forty minutes, weaving his Lexus in and out of traffic at speeds rarely reached on Long Island's congested highways. If a cop were to stop Ice, he'd find a .40 caliber pistol and Glock-9 under the passenger seat, as well as some coke and weed in the center console. It would be enough to get his probation violated and likely send him back to prison for a few years. It might also save him from whatever fate awaits him tonight. But there's no traffic stop or arrest. Not a single cop car in sight.

Ice is going so fast—his mind running through all his possible moves in response to the stash robbery—that he overshoots the Hempstead exit, ending up in Queens. He gets off the highway and stops at a bodega to buy Newports, chain-smoking them while pacing up and down the sidewalk outside the store. He mentally ticks off his options, none of which are good: He could gather up what remains of his set and wage an all-out assault on the Crips clubhouse; stake out Tyrek's apartment and assassinate him when he shows up; relocate his crew to new corners far from Crips territory; or walk away like his aunt had begged him to. Just keep driving to Manhattan, pick up I-95, and be in Atlanta the next day.

"Might be nice down there," he says.

It might also be the smartest choice. An assault on the Crips clubhouse or hit on Tyrek would be a boon to the Bloods, Ice knows, but their triumph would likely be short-lived. The Crips chain of command remains intact, meaning Tyrek's death would simply thrust Tony into the role of set leader, with Rock as his second-in-command. Those two, he knows, would never quit fighting. Continuing to go head-to-head with the Crips, Ice thinks, will likely lead to his death, as well as those of his remaining soldiers.

On the other hand, keeping the war going would salvage the Bloods' reputation. Ice knows what people in the neighborhood are saying about him and his set: They're punks and cowards; their leader ran off and hid when things got too hot. If legacies matter—and part of Ice thinks they do—he must keep blazing at his rival gang until all of his men, or all of theirs, are dead. That's the gangster in him talking, the man who took a broke-down Bloods set and, with the help and coke connections of his friend Steed, turned them into one of the strongest gangs in the region.

Ice had made them rich, street-famous, and dangerous. But as things stood now, they'd be remembered as cowards who backed down from a fight when the war's momentum turned against them. That's the legacy that awaits Ice, too, should he choose to relocate his operation to another neighborhood or escape to Atlanta. He wonders if he can live with that kind of reputation in the neighborhood.

He lights another Newport and thinks of Atlanta: the sun, the pretty young sisters, a thriving black business community that would probably welcome him with open arms, despite his record. It's a chance to do the right thing with his life, a chance to stay out of prison and reconnect with Cheryl, the only person left who still loves him. With the money he'd saved up from drug proceeds, he wouldn't even need the start-up capital she'd promised him. He could probably obtain the needed business licenses through her husband's connections and be up and running with his accounting firm in a few months.

Maybe he'd even stop by a few youth centers to talk to at-risk kids about gang life; how he'd lived it, escaped it, and found success. While he's at it, he might even find himself a fine-looking wife, get treatment for his PTSD, go get that master's in finance.

"Might be *real* nice," he says.

Yes, starting over was the smart thing to do, a chance to resume the path he should have stayed on all along. Honest work over quick riches. The embrace of real family over gang family. The pursuit of happiness over desire for revenge, money, and reputation as the hardest gangster in town.

He's weighing the pros and cons of this plan—oblivious to what's happening in the bodega behind him—when the clerk leaves his post at the register. Ice doesn't see him walk into the rear stock room and make a phone call, doesn't know he's one of a handful of Queens informants the Crips pay to supply them information. When a white SUV turns onto the block and parks near the bodega, Ice doesn't notice that, either. He's too lost in thought, imagining all the possibilities for his future. Only the sound of high heels clicking on the sidewalk behind him stirs Ice from his revelry.

"This for sticking your boys on me, you sick mothafucka," Leticia says, firing a single shot into the back of Ice's head.

Once again, there's only one king in town.

CHAPTER SIXTEEN

Hot Spots

There's an army of walking wounded, kids whose bodies are totally broken before they turn twenty-one.

—Detective Delahunt

When the clock strikes midnight on January 1, 2013, one of the bloodiest years in Hempstead's history comes to an end. Village police tallied forty shooting victims in 2012, more than any year except 2007, when police reported forty-three victims—many of them Bloods and Crips—being shot. The statistics, per capita, rank Hempstead among the most dangerous suburban municipalities in the country. In total, fifty-six people in the region were shot in connection with the Triangle war in 2012, most of them gang members.[1] Ten died. Three were fully or partially paralyzed. Dozens of others attend rehabilitation facilities throughout the metropolitan area, learning to use their wounded muscles again, trying to overcome the pain and trauma of gunshot injuries.

"There's an army of walking wounded, kids whose bodies are totally broken before they turn twenty-one," says Delahunt. "And that's just one gang war. Add up all your Bloods-Crips beefs throughout the country, and you've got a whole generation of these broken-down kids."

Nonfatal Triangle war casualties are usually left to convalesce at New York City hospitals specializing in long-term treatment for

---

[1] Final victim total is based on police and court records, as well as interviews with gang members and gunshot victims.

gunshot victims. Many live at Coler-Goldwater, a hospital and nursing facility on Roosevelt Island catering to poor, chronically ill patients. In Coler's corridors, Crips and Bloods once sworn to each other's destruction offer friendly nods when passing each other in wheelchairs pushed by health-care aides. A few are partially paralyzed. Some are blind from bullet fragments that sliced through their eyes. Others suffered internal injuries so severe they can't go more than a few hours without treatment.

"In here, all that stuff I cared about on the street don't matter anymore," says Rashawn Simon, a Hempstead Blood left paralyzed on his left side by a gang shooting in early 2012. "Now, I see Crips I hated back then, people I'd have shot like it was nothing, and I've got nothing but love for them. Because we're the only ones who understand each other's tragedies. We know what a waste all that was. Then, we were trying to be hard, trying to rep our hood. Now, we see each other sitting in wheelchairs and it's like, 'Damn, why the hell did we do all that?'"

One of Rashawn's former rivals, a partially paralyzed Crip named Jamal Pearson, is housed on the same floor. He says his favorite part of the day is wheeling out to one of the Roosevelt Island piers with Rashawn and staring at the East River.

"I guess soldiers understand each other," Jamal says. "When they had a New Year's Eve party on our floor, we went outside to look at the river instead, because we couldn't handle all that. You know, 2013 is supposed to be a chance for people to start over. But for us, there's no starting over, because can't neither of us walk. They say it's a clean slate, but having done what we did in the Triangle, we don't get clean slates."

A regular visitor to their floor at Coler is Roberto Mello, the child who had two fingers blown off when a stray slug struck him as he lay in bed reading *The Cat in the Hat*. Roberto comes to the hospital twice weekly for physical therapy, so that he might one day be able to effectively use his injured hand.

"I can't use it the way I used to because of the Bloods and Crips," says Roberto, nine. "That's why we moved out of Hempstead, because their fighting hurt me."

For gangsters who remain in Hempstead, the Triangle war also left an indelible mark. Each says they changed dramatically during the conflict, having seen their friends killed and horrifically wounded, suffering their own gunshot or stab wounds, and doling out cruelties some hadn't thought themselves capable of. Coming of age amid a gang war, they experienced the kind of fear and trauma unknown to most young men not fighting overseas. They'd also made the kind of money they once only dreamed about, demonstrating how the Bloods-Crips drug trade survives, even thrives, in a war economy.

"Compared to how my life was a year ago, everything's changed," says Bolo Jay. "I was a boy then. Now I'm a man, mos def. I've been shot at. I've seen my boys' wigs get split [by gunfire]. Saw a whole bunch of other niggas get popped, torn up by slugs, all types of nasty shit. But that's the game. The game make you grow up fast. Honestly, I can't even remember how I was before all this beefing started. I know I wasn't a soldier like I am now. Straight up, I'm a different person than I was."

The Crips Big Homies also saw their lives transformed by the gang war. Tyrek had begun 2012 as a relatively untested leader. His reputation as a smart, fierce player in the drug game had already earned him respect and accolades in the Long Island and New York City underworld. But because he'd never before led the Crips during wartime, gangland observers were uncertain of his ability to defeat the Bloods, keep up morale, and maintain supply lines during a full-scale conflict.

Now, his skeptics silenced and his drug operation expanding, Tyrek's a neighborhood legend. Little kids in the Triangle stand awestruck and wave at him as he drives through his territory—treatment typically reserved for famous athletes and movie stars. He says he eats his dinners at the best restaurants in New York City, spends each night with a different beautiful woman.

"I guess you could say my stock done rose since this shit started," Tyrek says. "I ain't going to tell you I'd been through anything like that [war] when we got into it, but you got to step up when the time comes. So I stepped up. That's my job. Everybody got a job, everybody got a role to play. It's like if you a general in war. That's the way I see myself.

"Every move I make, I got to be two steps ahead of my enemies. I need to know my people and understand their strengths and weaknesses so I know how to use them. Ain't no difference between leading troops out here or in the desert, mountains, wherever our army and marines be fighting. As far as my life go, I feel like I learned a lot about how to be a leader, how to make more money. I mean, I feel like I could do anything now. But ain't like I can get a real paying job with my record. I'm in this here game for life."

Tony, awaiting the birth of his second son, believes the war better prepared him for fatherhood. He has spent huge sums of drug proceeds on baby clothes, toys, games, diapers, and other supplies, all of them top of the line. The money he once blew on all-night parties, drugs, and prostitutes now goes mostly toward his son's wardrobe and sneaker collection.

"Because of [the war], I understand better that you can be here one minute, gone the next, so I need to appreciate every second with my kids," Tony says. "In the game, what's going to happen to you is going to happen regardless. If you going to get got, you going to get got. That's the life we chose, and it come with the territory. But all this fighting done made me realize even more how fragile life is. I could be gone tomorrow, so I need to cherish every second I get to spend with my son, and my other child when he comes.

"I'm definitely going to be a better pop to them because of all we been through on these streets. Just because their dad's got a little street fame don't mean I'm not going to be there for them."

Whereas the Crips became local celebrities after the Triangle war, Hempstead Bloods found themselves plunged into infamy. The machismo, bragging, and shit-talking inherent in being a Bloods member seemed harder to pull off in the wake of their loss, and it presents a question: If you've lost a gang war but still love your neighborhood and your set, how are you supposed to move on?

"I feel like I don't really know what my life's about right now," says J-Roc. "I want to keep fighting those Crip bitches, but I ain't got the back. Ain't enough niggas still around to go after them. But I want to *real* bad. Because I'm mad at the way they punked us. I feel embarrassed. When I go out, people talk all kinds of shit about how they done smoked our boys and took the territory we had. Was a time people talked that shit, we'd'a knocked they blocks off, too. But now? It's like we weak. And Ice, Steed, everybody gone. So who's going to lead? Maybe I need to step up."

In the early weeks of 2013, things are quieter between the Hempstead Crips and Bloods than at any time in recent memory. The once-constant rumors of reprisals have finally stopped circulating. The remaining Bloods, ashamed by their losses but unwilling to quit slinging, have moved outside the neighborhood to sell packages on consignment for other crews.

For long-suffering residents of the Triangle, the improvement seems almost unbelievable. Marsha Ricks says she feels as if she's living in an entirely different neighborhood. For the first time in years, she's sleeping with her bedroom window open, no longer fearful of stray bullets finding their way inside.

"I believe those gun battles are a thing of the past," she says. "I believe my prayers have been answered."

"This is what we've been fighting for," says Reverend Lyons. "This is why we march. Peace and quiet; you can't measure the importance of these things."

The police, too, hail their role in curbing gang shootings.

"We've made a real impact," says Michael McGowan, the Hempstead police chief.

But the quiet, they know, is mostly a result of the Triangle war's grim toll. Ice is dead from a gunshot wound. Steed's at a physical rehabilitation facility in New Jersey, where Marsha Ricks's son is helping him study for his GED. Doc, Ice's other lieutenant, has been in his grave nearly two months. Lamar, Ice's once-promising protégé, is buried in the same cemetery. So is Super Curt.

With those five out of the picture, Big Boy Owens is next in line to run the Bloods. But before he can begin his reign, he's arrested for gang assault at a party. That leaves only J-Roc, Spider Rick, a few second-string corner boys, and some elementary-school-age Bloods associates. All are young and inexperienced compared to their predecessors, and police quickly outmaneuver them. A well-planned sting operation leads to the busts of several on drug charges, including Rick.

"Ain't nobody left to fight, that's why it's quiet," says Tyrek. "One crew wins; the other crew walks away. That's how it goes in the hood."

In February, the Crips throw a victory party at an abandoned home in the Triangle. There's plenty of beer and liquor, a couple of guys cooking burgers on the grill out back, and abundant supplies of weed and coke for the victorious gangsters. They laugh, drink, and smoke without fear of shootings or fights. This, they know, is peacetime.

"We earned this shit right here," Tyrek tells Rock as they share a blunt.

"To the fullest," Rock says.

"End of the day, those niggas didn't have nothing for us, huh?"

"Not a damn thing."

"And Leticia came through like nobody's business," Tyrek says. "Girl's got a lot of heart. Got her some revenge."

After all the fighting and shooting, all the bloodshed and funerals, the MLK corners are rightfully theirs, Rock says. But despite their victory, there's something bothering him. They haven't seized the new territory, nor made the slightest move toward expanding in that direction. Rock wants to know why they went to all that trouble, paid such a high cost, if they're just going to let a couple of sorry-ass independent dealers move in to the Bloods territory they'd fought so hard for.

"Why don't we take them corners right now?" he says. "You said we earned this shit right here. Well, we earned them corners, too, all them corners. And we're just going to let these independent niggas move they weak-ass packages there? I don't understand that. What ain't I seeing?"

"You seeing everything," Tyrek says. "But it was never just about territory, yo. I mean, we'll send a crew out there next week or week after. Ain't no thang now. Nobody going to fuck with us when we come through. Those independent niggas will go quietly."

"Aight, so we going to take the territory, but we ain't really give a fuck about it? I mean, why run them slobs off then, if we wasn't all about them corners?"

"Because they stepped to us, yo. Simple as that."

"Word? That all?"

"Yo, you know better than anybody. They came out all chest-thumping, like they was going take the Triangle and shit, so of course we had to come down hard on them niggas. Nah, we ain't need their corners. But once they came at us, that territory was going to be ours. *Had* to be. Ain't nobody come at us without paying the price. Plus, they was Bloods, nigga. We born to kill those slobs."

"I feel you," Rock says. "Serves as a warning to all these other weak-ass sets. A deterrent."

"Exactly, yo," Tyrek says. "A mothafucking deterrent to the fullest."

Despite the slowdown in violence, Lyons and his marchers work through the winter months in Hempstead. No matter the temperature, they're at least a dozen strong every week. By now, everyone in the neighborhood—from the pipeheads and slingers to the cops and prostitutes—knows them by name. Most Friday nights are quiet, the marchers finding fewer addicts stumbling through the Triangle, fewer gangsters casting menacing glances at each other.

"The problem's still here," Calvin Bishop says. "But it's not a war. And for that, we thank God."

They see other positive signs: more police patrolling the Triangle and MLK; more residents sitting on their stoops or lawn chairs outside their homes; and more kids running around outside their buildings, their parents comfortable enough to let them wander a little farther than usual.

"It really is getting better," says Bishop. "You can see it. You can sense it when you walk around. People are feeling more confident, feeling . . . hopeful. And hope is something that can change lives. I mean, this is the reason some of us, myself included, wanted to march . . . to make up for what we did when we were young, men running wild around here. I feel like I'm making up for some of that pain I caused through my drug use, through all my stupidity. This is why we've been out here every week—to achieve this progress."

A few of the gangsters, too, show appreciation for Lyons and the dedication of his marchers. The fact that they've come through every

Friday night to pray with the hustlers, regardless of weather, family commitments, or ongoing gunplay, means something to the young men. For many, Lyons and his marchers are the only positive male figures in their lives, their own fathers having died from gangs or drugs, or imprisoned because of them.

Lyons says some of the gangsters send him "messages through the grapevine, that they appreciate us coming out in the middle of the night and praying for them. In the beginning, they were very confrontational. Now when they see us, they either run if they don't want to pray, or they put down whatever they're doing and join hands with us on the street corners, praying and expressing their gratitude for us being out there, and, in their own words, showing them some love."

Clary and Delahunt are also feeling more confident about the chances for peace, at least in the short term. Over weekly dinners, the marine supplies the detective with intelligence about gang activity he sees in the Triangle and MLK. Tonight, they toast to the apparent end of the gang war, to the prayer marchers, and to themselves, for sticking around long enough to see the shooting stop.

"I couldn't believe my eyes in the Triangle today," Clary says. "I'm walking up in there, then to MLK, and it's dead quiet. I thought I was dreaming, man. And then, what almost made my jaw drop was the sight of these two little girls playing in the water spraying out a hose they'd turned on in the project courtyard. Even before I went to Iraq, I'd never seen that on MLK before."

"I know what you mean," Delahunt says. "Feels like a different place. I keep waiting for all hell to break loose down there, but right now, it's not looking like that."

"It actually feels kind of *safe*," Clary says.

"Safe," says Delahunt.

The men bask in the word, as if it will redeem them, along with all the carnage they've witnessed. Clary repeats it again, as though the word itself is a reward for all those nights his mother prohibited him from going outside when he was a kid, because the gangs—forerunners of the Crips and Bloods—were beefing again. He'd lived through those old gang wars and tried to limit the carnage wrought by the new one. But neither he nor Delahunt is foolish enough to believe this new crop of gangsters would ever put down their guns for good.

"What I want to know is this," Clary says. "How the hell did we go from seeing bodies dropping on the regular to folks all but singing 'Kumbaya' out on them corners? They take out *every one* of them Bloods boys?"

"Just about," Delahunt says. "Most of their leaders got killed. One of them left town and hasn't been seen for months. We nailed a few others, built a couple of good cases. Perfect storm, you could say."

"They going to come back? Regroup?"

"Maybe, but I don't see how at the moment. There's no one left to put the crew back together. Most of the Bloods left out here are the younger members. They're not married to the game as a business the way the older players were. So they don't have the incentive to put their necks on the line and keep beefing with the guys who already ran them off."

"Peace," Clary says.

"Beautiful, isn't it?"

"For now."

＊＊＊

There are new problems for Delahunt and his colleagues to deal with as February draws to a close: beefs between Hempstead's Latin American gangs, turf disputes between independent dealers, and an influx of illegal guns flooding the streets, all leading to a surge in armed domestic disputes and fistfights-turned-shootings.

Whereas the Triangle's abandoned homes and MLK's project buildings served as epicenters of violence in 2012, shootings and knifings in the first months of 2013 are more common on the blocks around Seduccion, the strip club where Ice and his set once held strategy sessions. Reverend Lyons, satisfied that violence in the Triangle has been quelled for the time being, turns his attention to preventing shootings in and around the club, holding demonstrations with other antiviolence activists calling for an end to the bloodshed.

"It's not a Crips and Bloods thing at this club or in some of these other communities experiencing violence, but the underlying issues—poverty, easy access to guns, lack of positive role models—remain the same," Lyons says. "Wherever violence spreads, whether it's gang-related or otherwise, we have a duty to try and help. I wish we had less to do, but that's simply not the world we live in."

As cops and activists flock to new hot spots, the Crips begin expanding their operations, opening more corners throughout Long Island and New York City. They operate with a freedom—from both police pressure and Bloods threats—unseen since before the Triangle war.

"Sounds like they got bigger problems than us," Tyrek says of the cops.

Some of the remaining Bloods take note of the police absence, too. J-Roc, who has been spending his postwar days getting high and playing Xbox, rolls through his crew's old territory one night and sees MLK devoid of a single cop car. When the Triangle comes into view, there are Crips dealing out in the open, no five-o's in sight.

"What the fuck?" J-Roc says. "Maybe it's time to go back to work."

He calls up a few of his friends from Freeport—members of another Bloods set anxious to move into new markets. He tells them about the peace that's broken out in his neighborhood and the opportunity it represents. They tell him they've heard all about how his crew got beat down by the Crips, but that he shouldn't worry.

"We got mad product out here and not enough good corners," one of the Freeport Bloods, Fly Carl, tells him. "I'll come down there with some homies next week. If it looks promising, we'll split a package with you and whatever niggas you got left who ready to work."

"Hells yeah," J-Roc says. "That's what I'm talking about."

A few days later, Spider Rick and Big Boy, both locked up following recent police operations, accept no-jail plea deals. J-Roc's waiting for them in the courthouse when they're freed.

"You all ready to grind?" he says.

"Yeah, yo," says Big Boy. "To the fullest."

"Aight then. We back in business."

CHAPTER SEVENTEEN

Death Day

It's a free country.

—J-Roc

In anticipation of heading back to their old corners, and possibly mounting a fresh challenge to the Crips, J-Roc and his newly freed cohorts call for a "Death Day" celebration to boost morale. On what would have been Ice's fifth anniversary as set leader, they throw a party—a remembrance not just for their fallen gang boss, but for all the homies they lost in the Triangle war.

More than two hundred people show up, mostly Bloods members, their friends, and girls from MLK. They gather in the backyard of a vacant house just outside the Triangle, sipping cups of Hennessy in honor of Ice. They wear shirts with his photograph emblazoned on the front and share stories about Bloods hustlers who recently died in battle.

Blown-up photos of fallen soldiers are also propped up on wooden easels for people to sign. The deceased gangsters' closets have been emptied by their gang brothers, who lay out matching outfits on the ground as a way to memorialize the men.

"I think about you every day because you was the one who taught me how to be a man," J-Roc writes on a photo of Ice. "For real, Ice, your name will ring out here forever."

Spider Rick, taking the pen from J-Roc, writes down some rap lyrics he'd composed in Ice's memory.

Nigga you was the illest
By any measure the realest
Your life was too damn important
For them bitches to steal it

When he's done, Rick wipes a tear from his eye and explains to a girl he'd brought to the party why Ice was so important to him.

"Baby, you should know who this nigga was, because he was the realest hustler I ever met," Rick says. "He was rich and shit, was a real businessman, but he gave it up to come back and run these corners. That's a true soldier right there . . . somebody who had a tight setup and all kinds of legitimate cash, but still wouldn't turn his back on his people."

"But if he had all that, a good job and money, why'd he come back?" the girl asks. "He must've known he was probably going to get killed. Tyrek's people don't play."

"Bitch, don't be talking that mess," Rick says, slapping her on the mouth.

She runs off crying as several Bloods who heard the exchange laugh and point at her.

"Girl needs to show some respect," Rick tells them.

On the other side of the yard, a few Freeport Bloods hang Ice's red Miami Heat jersey on a nearby clothesline. Each of them caresses it, whispering a message to him.

"You ain't never going to be forgotten, yo," one of the Bloods says. "You gave your life for your set, died for your niggas. That's for real, yo. Mad respect. Wish you peace and eternal rest."

A Brooklyn Bloods leader says a prayer for Ice's soul while rubbing the jersey. Then he genuflects and tells his fellow gangsters, some of them new Bloods, that Ice's behavior during the last few hours of his life was the ultimate example of gang loyalty.

"A lot of niggas would've run away instead of coming back, knowing they was probably going to get dropped," he says. "But this nigga Ice wasn't about to go out like no punk. That's how we do. That's how you got to be . . . willing to sacrifice for your boys until the end. And that's how you get yourself a Death Day. This here reserved for the true hustlers."

Death Day celebrations are indeed rare in Hempstead. As such, they tend to be treated like holy rites, similar to gatherings held by families and friends of suicide bombers who sacrifice their lives in the name of jihad. The lives of deceased gang members are never the focus of Death Day gatherings. Rather, their demise is what the attendees dwell on, analyze, and celebrate. Death, when it comes in service of the set, is to be extolled, glorified. At these gatherings, martyrdom is treated with the utmost reverence. To attain such an end is to be a hero forever in the eyes of one's gang brothers.

"It's the greatest honor," says J-Roc.

The mythology of Ice's death builds as the celebration wears on, story by story, prayer by prayer. He's continuously revered, recalled as a hero and martyr for the Bloods' cause. None of the partygoers know of the decision he'd apparently made just before his death to flee Hempstead and start anew in Atlanta. If they did, perhaps they'd call him a coward who'd been too scared to stay and fight—the worst thing that can be said about a fellow gangster.

But Ice, in the collective memory of these streets, would never be marked as such. The legacy he'd fretted over in the hours before his murder is secure—one of a selfless soldier and great leader, the kind of gangster who would serve as an example to young hustlers for years to come.

"I'm'a be just like you," J-Roc says, eyeing Ice's photograph. "Get it on till I die."

After three hours, cops arrive and break up the celebration. The crowd moves to the home of a Bloods associate in Roosevelt to continue their festivities. Once again, they set up the memorial photos and display Ice's jerseys, hats, and sneakers. It's two-thirty in the morning when J-Roc and his just-sprung-from-jail Bloods cohorts—feeling brave from copious amounts of weed and liquor—decide to roll through Crips territory and send a message. They want it known that the bloodletting of the past year has not destroyed their set. They need to show that, though they may be fewer in number now, they are not defeated.

Pictured here, a Crips drug corner where J-Roc pulls a gun on an enemy corner boy

KEVIN DEUTSCH

They pile into J-Roc's Grand Am, which a pipehead had traded to him a day earlier for $100 worth of crack, and drive into the Triangle. Right away they spot two Crips dealers on a corner and pull up. One of the Crips steps up to serve them.

"What you need?" the corner boy says.

"Need you to suck my dick," J-Roc says, pulling out a .357 Magnum revolver and pointing it at the kid. His face goes pale. J-Roc pulls the trigger as the boy closes his eyes and grimaces, anticipating a bullet. But the gun only clicks, its chamber empty. J-Roc lets out a big laugh. Big Boy and Rick crack up as well. Their glee only increases when they see a wet spot spreading across the front of the dealer's jeans.

"Nigga pissed his pants!" Big Boy says.

The humiliated kid backs slowly away from the Grand Am as his partner on the corner walks over to see what all the laughing's about. J-Roc speeds away, still giggling.

"Y'all some sorry-ass mothafuckas," he yells, flashing a Bloods hand sign as they head back to MLK. High on their triumph, they roll three fat blunts and crack open a bottle of Hennessy outside the Park Lake apartments. J-Roc phones Fly Carl, who drives over with his crew to partake in the celebration and talk about the possibility of splitting a package. They're all stoned, laughing over the encounter with the Crips corner boy, when J-Roc proposes a partnership between the sets.

"From what we seen tonight, those boys weak on some of their corners," J-Roc says. "They got more territory now than they got good soldiers to work it. So that's an opportunity for us. Them corners begging to get took."

"Yeah, yo, but ain't that how you all got into this situation in the first place?" Carl says. "By trying to take territory from those niggas in the Triangle?"

J-Roc seems caught off guard by the question. He admits he hadn't thought about it like that until now. It's true, he says, that the Triangle war had begun with the same kind of idea he's now proposing.

"Except we going to win this time," J-Roc says.

"Man, you all need to put some more thought into this," Carl says. "This ain't a time for acting a fool and rushing into some shit without thinking it through."

Carl and his crew thank their Hempstead brethren for the weed, say their good-byes, and head back to Freeport.

"Those little niggas be tripping," Carl says on the drive home.

J-Roc, rolling another blunt, says he's undiscouraged by Carl's skepticism. If he doesn't want to tool up and show the Crips what they're about, he'll find some boys who do.

"Yo, what happened to that nigga D-Bo?" J-Roc says. "We could use him about now."

They'd all but forgotten about Devon, their newest initiate. None of them could recall seeing him since before the ambush on Ice, Steed, and Super Curt.

"I heard he was about to go off to college in Carolina or something," says Big Boy.

"Shit, he ain't going no place but with us," J-Roc says. "Let's go get his ass."

They drive to Devon's house and ring the doorbell. A few moments later, they hear people arguing inside. A woman unlocks the door but keeps it chained as she peeks through the crack.

"Devon home?" asks Big Boy.

"No," the woman says. She is pretty but tired-looking, her face so much like Devon's that the Bloods know right away she's his mother. "He's moved away."

"Where to?" Big Boy asks.

"I don't know," she says.

"What you mean, you don't know?" asks J-Roc. "How you ain't know where your own son moved to?"

"He ran away from home. That's all I know."

She starts to close the door, but J-Roc stops it with the heel of his Air Jordan.

"He didn't run away," says J-Roc. "I heard him before you came to the door. He's inside."

"Boy, get your foot off my door this second."

"Tell Devon to come outside then," Rick says.

"I told you he's gone! Now get out of here."

"Nah, we ain't leaving without Devon," says J-Roc, reaching toward his waist.

He presses his sneaker harder against the door, the chain lock beginning to buckle under the pressure.

"Please go," Toni LaFleur says, sounding scared for the first time now. Just then a siren blares in the street. The Bloods turn and see Delahunt in his car, looking more pissed-off than usual.

"Get the hell off her property," he shouts. "Now."

"Damn," J-Roc says, taking his foot off the door. Devon's mom immediately slams it shut, and Delahunt summons the boys. They swagger over to his car with affected limps, doing their best impressions of Ice. The deceased Bloods leader walked that way only because Marvin shot him in his leg. These boys are able-bodied, can walk straight as they please, but think the limp-strut makes them look tough, like their idol.

"What are you knuckleheads doing bothering Ms. LaFleur?" Delahunt says. "You all got no reason to be over here."

"It's a free country," J-Roc says.

"It ain't going to be free for your little ass much longer if you keep it up," Delahunt says.

"We wasn't doing nothing wrong," says Big Boy. "We just looking for Devon is all. You seen him?"

Delahunt had seen Devon, but doesn't dare mention that, fearing these boys are out to harm him. After Ice's murder, Devon's mom called him, begging him to help get her son out of town before he wound up dead. The detective rushed over and wrote her a check to cover Devon's airfare to South Carolina, helped her pack a suitcase for her son, and even agreed to drive him to the airport.

They booked Devon's flight for the following month, since his aunt wouldn't be back from vacationing in Myrtle Beach for another few weeks. Delahunt ordered Devon not to leave the house until the day of the flight, a command seconded by his mother. And he'd mostly gone along with the prohibition, only sneaking out for some fresh air in the early mornings when most hustlers are asleep.

When J-Roc, Big Boy, and Spider Rick showed up at his door that night, Devon was just about ready to leave town. His flight was scheduled for the next morning. All he'd needed was to get through one more night and he'd be home-free. The arrival of the three Bloods so shocked and terrified his mother that she ordered Devon to go hide in the bathroom, a plan he told her was silly. They argued over what to do next in hushed tones, but the Bloods heard them anyway.

"I *know* D-Bo's up in there," Big Boy tells Delahunt. "Why his mom tripping, lying to us like that?"

"Devon's long gone, from what I heard," Delahunt says. "Ain't anybody lying to you. She's just upset her son ran off. Now get out of here before I take you all in."

The Bloods saunter off toward J-Roc's Grand Am and watch Delahunt drive away. They're certain they'd heard Devon's voice in the house and vow to return later. In the meantime, they head to J-Roc's mom's place to play Call of Duty on Xbox. Stoned and tired, they fall asleep in his room, awakening just after eight the next morning.

"Let's go see if that nigga D-Bo still hiding out," J-Roc says.

When they pull up outside the LaFleurs' house this time, Devon is walking out the front door with his suitcase, believing the car he hears groaning up the block is Delahunt's, arriving to take him to the airport.

"Oh no," Devon says when he sees the Grand Am.

He drops his suitcase and takes off running toward his backyard, the three Bloods jumping out of the car to give chase. Devon jumps a fence and sprints as fast as he can, but his pursuers are single-minded. Block by block, they close in on him, darting through busy intersections and dodging cars.

As they near the Hempstead Long Island Rail Road Station, a group of boys standing just beyond the station parking lot point and stare at the four Bloods barreling toward them. Devon doesn't yet realize he's taken the worst possible route to elude his pursuers, for the corner he's approaching is one of the new Crips corners, opened as part of the set's postwar expansion.

The three Crips staffing the train station drug market—Bolo Jay, Savant Sharpe, and Dice Beckles—have been hearing rumors about some kind of Bloods' resurgence. So when they see Devon, J-Roc, Big Boy, and Spider Rick heading for them, they prepare for battle.

Bolo fingers the Glock in his waistband and asks his colleagues what to do.

"They probably coming to try and jack our stash," Savant says. "You got iron?"

Bolo nods, takes out the gun, and switches off its safety. Devon picks up his speed, buoyed by the sight of a train arriving in the distance. Drawing closer to the station, he finally recognizes the boys milling beside the lot just ahead. Devon sees Bolo raise his arm, glimpses a flash of chrome in his palm.

He tries to change direction but it's too late. A bullet strikes his side, the hot lead making a sizzling sound against his skin as he stumbles to the pavement. The Bloods turn and run, while the Crips sprint off the opposite way. Devon lay still in the street until a commuter spots him there and dials 911.

Delahunt, who'd been waiting for Devon outside his house, is the first cop to arrive. He jumps out of his car and immediately sees the bullet hole in Devon's abdomen. He kneels beside the kid's face and sees his eyes are open, full of tears.

"You hear me, Devon?"

"Yes."

"Don't move," he says as an ambulance arrives. "Just be still. They'll take care of you."

"I can't," Devon says.

"You can't what?"

"I can't feel anything."

The paramedics carefully roll Devon on his side, slide a stretcher under him, and load him into the ambulance. At the hospital, he explains the absence of feeling in his lower extremities, and doctors say they fear his spinal cord may have been damaged. A few days later, those fears are confirmed. Devon's told he might never walk again.

"I almost made it," he tells his mother as she sits on the edge of his hospital bed, stroking his forehead. "Almost."

CHAPTER EIGHTEEN

True to the Game

You've got to know when to give up . . . when a place is killing you.
—MIKE CLARY

Tyrek and Tony sit smoking blunts in the Crips clubhouse, discussing how to deal with Devon's shooting. They know the cops, especially Delahunt, are searching intensely for the gunman. They also believe one or more commuters at the train station may be able to identify the Crips who ran from the scene.

"Detectives already been by Bolo's crib," says Tony. "Somebody must've seen him run off. Or might be they got him on a surveillance camera."

"What the fuck he thinking, opening up on that weak-ass nigga D-Bo in the middle of the day and shit?" says Tyrek.

"Bolo thought Devon and them Bloods was coming to jack they stash," says Tony. "Turns out they was actually chasing Devon because he was dodging them and shit. But Bolo ain't know that, so he panicked, squeezed one off."

"Where he at now?"

"He up in our safe house in Brooklyn," Tony says. "But it seem like five-o ain't going to quit till they find his ass. Devon's mom making all kinds of noise about wanting justice and shit. Police coming down hard on our people, jacking up our corners, saying they going to keep on with all that until Bolo turn himself in."

Tyrek takes a deep pull off his blunt, considering his options. He doesn't want to lose his young hitter-in-training, but business takes precedence. If Bolo's freedom means an unacceptable level of police focus on Crips corners, then he can't stay free.

"Aight, tell him he got to put in for [the shooting]," says Tyrek. "Tell him we'll take care of his little bro while he in, take care of the money for his lawyer, everything. When he comes out, long as he do his time like a soldier, he's going to have a bigger piece of the pie. My word on that."

Tyrek's order is not out of the ordinary. Crips and Bloods leaders have long been known to sacrifice a soldier in the short term if it's beneficial to the set. The tricky part, Tyrek says, comes when detectives start making them promises in return for testimony or information about the gang.

"Make sure he's clear on his responsibilities," Tyrek says. "He keeps his got-damn mouth shut. He stay true to the game."

"Aight, I'll go get him," says Tony. "What you want to do with his corner in the meantime? You want another soldier on that?"

"Nah, forget that corner," Tyrek says. "With all this heat, we ain't got to push things local. We going to open some more of them city corners."

"We on that multimillion-dollar plan now, huh?" says Tony.

"No doubt," Tyrek says. "Bills about to get even larger."

An hour later, Tony's sitting down with Bolo at the safe house, explaining that he must turn himself in for the good of the gang.

"But how's that good for us?" Bolo says. "How having me in jail going to help us? I thought I was doing good."

"You was," Tony says. "You a soldier for real. You showed a lot of heart. But that ain't got nothing to do with you putting in for this [shooting]."

Bolo looks as if he's about to cry. He lowers his head, sniffles a few times.

"I still don't get it," he says.

"This just the way it is, yo," Tony says. "You down for your niggas, so you do what you've got to do. Too many cops on our corners looking for you right now, and it's bad for business. You go in, it takes the heat off us."

"But then I got to go to jail, right?"

"Probably," Tony says. "And you'll carry that like a soldier, too. You ain't going to tell them detectives shit about shit. They going to ask you all about our business, make you all kinds of promises to keep you out of jail if you snitch, but you ain't going to say a got-damn thing. 'Cause you down for your crew, right?"

"Yeah," says Bolo. "But I ain't never been to jail before."

"You get used to it real quick," Tony says. "We getting you a pay lawyer who going to get you as little time as possible, maybe get you down from attempted murder to assault and a weapons charge, depending on what kind of witnesses they got. So you hooked up on that front. And when you get out, Tyrek says he's promoting you. Going to double what you making now. Plus, he going to take care of your little bro Alex while you away. Clothes, cash, whatever he needs, we'll get to him."

With this last caveat, Bolo seems to resign himself to the situation. He meets his lawyer at a diner near the police station to talk strategy, with Tony manning the door to make sure Bolo doesn't make a run for it.

That night, in county lockup, Bolo makes a vow to leave the criminal justice system "twice as hard a hustler" as he is going in. "It'll make me tougher," he says. "When I get out, ain't no Blood going to want no part of me. And one day, I'm going to be in charge of all this shit. I'm going to be like Tyrek, the king, the number-one nigga in Hempstead. I'll show all these Bloods niggas what I'm about. Shit, I'll jail like it ain't nothing. Jail ain't going to do shit to me but prepare me to swallow all them Bloods niggas up when I get on the street again with my nine."

❧

Back in the Triangle, Reverend Lyons and his marchers return to try and tamp down the talk of renewed warfare. He keeps working to impact the lives of gang members he's met, to help them find better paths for their lives. But he still doesn't know when the next homicide will come, or how the local Bloods–Crips conflict might be permanently solved.

"It's an uphill battle," Lyons says. "We believe these young men are capable of so much more than what they're doing out here."

For every gang member the marchers have influenced over the past year, it seems that many others have ignored their message. Skinny Pete says praying with the men each Friday night has had a powerful impact on him, sparking his interest in theology and making him consider swearing off all violence.

"Sometimes, when I think about all I've done to niggas, I'm ashamed," Pete says. "I feel that way more and more 'cause I got prayer in my life now, because of the reverend. He made me see things differently."

In the other camp are unrepentant gangsters like Savant Sharpe, who's still convinced Lyons and his marchers are working for the police. He's written rap lyrics declaring the men "snitches and slobs [Bloods] lovers." Whenever he sees them, he walks off in the other direction and tries to calm his temper, "because if I don't, them Jesus-loving niggas might get hurt."

In Lyons's view, his marches have been a success—instrumental to the slowdown in gang-related gunplay. He attributes this partially to the efforts that he and his colleagues have made, and partially to the grace of God. But as a preacher born to these streets, he's not so naive as to think the gang war is over for good. He knows that, in all likelihood, he'll once again be summoned into the breach.

"When it's time to come back and march again," Lyons says, "we'll be here. We've put in too much time, too much effort, to give up on these young men."

But one hustler the marchers had no choice but to give up on was Tyrek. He'd once told Calvin Bishop he didn't mind the activists coming through the Triangle to pray, but that "if we ever interrupted him in the course of his doing business, no quarter would be given to us," Bishop says. "He said murder was nothing to him, and that the Lord has no say in it. That young man has too much of the Devil in him to be saved, I'm afraid."

Tyrek is rarely seen in the Triangle during the early months of 2013, having shifted many of his resources and best talent to New York City now that the Triangle, in his words, "has been locked up permanently as our stronghold." His crews are running several corners in Brooklyn and

Queens, tapping into brand-new markets and doubling their profits in the process.

But with new territory comes new enemies. Tyrek's men are already making a few in East New York, Brooklyn, and Jamaica, Queens. A member of one Brooklyn crew, the Very Crispy Gangsters, shoots a Hempstead Crip in the shoulder over a turf dispute in March. In response to a different territory grab in Jamaica, a notoriously violent Queens crew called the Get Touched Boys sends a group of gangsters to retake a corner from the Crips. They jump out of a car holding baseball bats, tire irons, and pistols. Before the Crips lookouts and touts know what's happening, some of the GTB gangsters are beating them while others train guns in their direction. The Crips are carrying but have no time to draw. Their rivals pummel them, bloodying their noses, pounding their skulls with gun barrels. Still, the Queens crew does not relent. They kick the ribs and faces of the Crips, the sound of bones cracking audible amid the scrum.

"It was ugly," Tony says after the attack, icing a black eye. "That's the cost of doing business sometimes."

The Crips relocate to another corner a few blocks up the street, outside the Get Touched Boys' territory. The change appears to satisfy GTB. Within a week, the Crips are making as much selling crack there as they had in the original spot.

"More than enough territory to go around in New York, because everybody need they fix on any block in any neighborhood," Tyrek says. "You just bring the product, and customers will find you. We can all get paid—Crip, GTB, whatever."

The Very Crispy Gangsters, though, are not as easy to appease. The crew's members are known as fierce protectors of their Brooklyn turf, and when Tyrek refuses to withdraw from a corner his crew took from VCG three weeks earlier, VCG takes the battle to Hempstead. In the heart of the Triangle, they beat down a Crips corner crew, humiliating them on their own turf. The move is brazen and, Tyrek believes, foolish.

"They don't know who they're dealing with," Tyrek says. "They think we soft 'cause we ain't from Brooklyn. But we going to show them niggas something about how we do in Hempstead."

In response to the beating, Tyrek dispatches Rock and two soldiers to shoot up a VCG corner. The mission is only a partial success, leaving two gangsters wounded, but neither fatally. The VCG response, on the other hand, is highly effective. They reach out to J-Roc through an intermediary and form a temporary alliance with the remaining Hempstead Bloods, both crews seeing the benefit in teaming up to fight a common enemy. Within hours of the agreement, J-Roc drives past a Crips corner in Brooklyn and opens fire, killing Flex Butler.

"How you like us now?" he says while speeding away.

Flex, the third-highest-ranking Crip in the set's hierarchy, lay in the gutter for over half an hour, his body obscured by the shadows cast by nearby project towers. A local pipehead stumbles upon the body and rifles through Flex's pockets, coming away with several bags of premium crack. Only after he smokes one of the rocks does he bother calling 911.

The murder sets off a new wave of violence at a time when Hempstead residents believed their neighborhood's fortunes had finally improved. As VCG and Bloods soldiers wage a campaign of force and intimidation against Tyrek's men, the staccato sound of gunshots once again becomes frequent in the Triangle. The Crips, caught off guard by their foes' partnership, call for reinforcements and additional weapons from affiliate sets in Brooklyn and Queens.

"They brought the fight to us," Rock says. "We didn't expect it."

The resurgent Bloods, led by J-Roc, Big Boy, and Rick, see the campaign as an opportunity to improve their own credibility and reputations in Hempstead after last year's embarrassments. A few of them catch Dice Beckles alone on his way home from a corner shift and beat him down, shouting out insults about the Crips while pummeling him. Next, they rape a female pipehead who's friendly with Tyrek.

"That's payback," says J-Roc, who admits to taking part in the sexual assault. "She ran with them punks, so she got to pay the price."

The barrage of shootings, rapes, and beatings sow confusion among the Crips. When under attack, they're sometimes unsure whether VCG or Bloods are doing the shooting—and therefore unclear about who should be targeted for retaliation.

More significantly, the three-way gang war is affecting the set's bottom line. Tyrek's losing profits both on his Brooklyn corners, where customers are afraid to cop due to the constant threat of gunfire, as well as his Hempstead corners, now under siege. Under pressure from soldiers who have seen their pay drastically reduced in recent weeks, he decides to withdraw from VCG territory and relocate to unclaimed turf, just as he'd successfully done in Queens.

"I don't want to back off, but sometimes that's got to be part of the strategy," he says. "It's . . . how you call it? . . . A tactical withdrawal."

The withdrawal, however, does not satisfy VCG. They continue to harass and attack Crips corner crews even after they relocate as far as Flatbush and Bedford-Stuyvesant. And they keep up their incursions into Hempstead, ripping off Crips stash houses, shooting up cookhouses, and tagging the set's exterior clubhouse walls with spray paint.

"Them niggas are tenacious," says Tony.

Tyrek says VCG's reputation is being bolstered by their battle with his set; the longer and harder they fight, the more they're seen as a major player in New York's gang hierarchy. Taking on a respected Crips set, and hurting them, is the dream of most every start-up crew unaffiliated with a national gang network, Tyrek says.

"That's why they ain't quitting, even though we gave them back their corners," he says. "They names ringing out now because they taking us on. They got a lot of street fame out of this."

<hr>

The renewal of hostilities again makes it unsafe to roam the Triangle after dark. For Marsha Ricks, the return of gunfire outside her door is almost too much to bear. If her spirits had been buoyed by the temporary peace, the resumption of violence saps her of energy and hope.

"I truly believed the neighborhood had finally turned a corner, that these boys had found a way to coexist," she says. "I was taking walks and shopping on my own for the first time in a long while. Shoot, I was even feeling a little younger, going to the beauty parlor once a week."

The violence has again left her trapped in her house, held hostage by the ongoing threat of stray bullets. Her health seems to be worsening, too, her body achier than usual. Perhaps she'd exerted herself too much during those peaceful weeks, she says. One night, she slips and falls in her bathroom, fracturing a bone in her leg. She crawls into the living room to reach her phone and call an ambulance, which whisks her to the hospital. When she returns home, it's in a wheelchair, her leg held in place by a stabilizing brace.

She finds it difficult to get around but refuses to burden her son with news of her injury. He's busy finishing up his residency while mentoring Steed, and she doesn't want him distracted at such an important time. She wheels through her home as best she can, calling on neighbors, including Mike Clary, to buy her groceries and run other errands. Once again, she sleeps with her windows closed.

Cooped up in her house every day, she grows weak and depressed. Her medical issues mount. But she still waxes nostalgic about a time in the Triangle before crack, Crips, and Bloods.

"There was a time, when I was growing up, when this was a beautiful place," she says. "I suppose my problem's always been that I *kept* seeing it that way, even after that world was long gone. Now I realize it isn't coming back."

The following month she suffers a major stroke as she lay in bed, the sound of gunfire crackling outside her window. Clary finds her the next day when he arrives to collect her grocery order. He checks her pulse, feels only cold stillness. He kisses her on the cheek and calls her son.

Clary is deeply affected by Ricks's death, believing it represents the end of the "old neighborhood," as well as a victory of evil over the forces of good that Ricks embodied.

"If we had a hundred more like her, we could have made this place good again," Clary says. "But she alone was a miracle. She kept me going many times when I didn't want to. A lot of us who wanted better things for this area feel . . . just kind of lost without her."

On the morning of Ricks's funeral, a stray bullet fired by J-Roc, still drunk and high from a night of partying, shatters the rear window of

Clary's car. When he comes home and finds the mess of shattered glass, he begins to cry right there in the street.

"Enough," he says.

He packs up his most important possessions, loads them into the car, and begins the long drive to Florida, where he plans to start fresh. He leaves shattered glass strewn about the car floor, hoping it will serve as a reminder of why he'd left—should he have any second thoughts.

Clary puts his house up for sale, but like so many others in the Triangle, it sits uninhabited and unmaintained, its windows quickly broken out by gangsters and junkies before village workers board them up.

"Best thing I ever did was leave," he'll say a year later, talking on the phone from a poolside lawn chair in Orlando, his wife, Diane, lying beside him. "You've got to know when to give up . . . when a place is killing you."

CHAPTER NINETEEN

The Takeaway

We want people to feel safe in their community. And we won't stop until they are. We owe that to them.

—Mayor Hall

When young men are able to wage war in suburban municipalities from Bridgeport, Connecticut, to Riviera Beach, Florida, when they're able to murder and rape without hesitation from Long Island to Westchester, perhaps it's time to accept that the Bloods-Crips battles of the last half-century—the street-corner assassinations, the drive-bys, the endless cycles of grief and retaliation—are not anomalies. They're part of an actual war, skirmishes in an armed conflict between street-hardened soldiers who've given up on the American dream. The gangsters realize this. The question is, when will everyone else?

"With all the criminal justice issues we're dealing with as a society, from drug legalization and sentencing reform to wrongful convictions and prison overcrowding, we seem to have lost interest in the Bloods-Crips conflict," says Delahunt. "All over America, folks take it for granted that the Crips and Bloods are going to kill each other, because that's 'just what they do.' We've been desensitized to this conflict, so that we somehow think it's normal that tens of thousands of young men, American men, have been at war for almost half a century because of the colors they wear."

Throughout the country, police officials, community groups, and antiviolence activists are still brainstorming ways to end Bloods-Crips conflicts. In the headquarters of suburban law enforcement agencies coast to coast—departments smaller and lesser-funded than their urban counterparts—cops are drawing up plans to try and stop the gangs from doing to their hometowns what they've done to Hempstead. And in their search for answers, they're turning their attention to the Triangle.

"What they have going on in Hempstead is a textbook feud between drug-dealing Bloods and Crips sets, so how that battle plays out in the long term has implications for all of us in suburban law enforcement," said a high-ranking police official in a suburb of Kansas City, Missouri, where Bloods and Crips are also warring. "In many ways, Hempstead is a testing ground for tactics to try and end the wider Bloods-Crips war."

In the LA suburbs of Inglewood and Santa Monica, where Bloods and Crips maintain strongholds, the Triangle war also serves as a case study for gang investigators looking to wipe out local drug markets.

"Hempstead's on the other side of the country, but we have the same types of problems with our Bloods and Crips as they do," says one Inglewood police official. "The future of suburban policing is beginning to look a lot more like urban policing because of these drug-dealing gangs making inroads. So we have to keep an eye on how other departments are handling what we call the 'urban creep' effect. And Hempstead's on the front lines of it."

So, what will it take to permanently end the war?

The answers aren't simple. Some police strategies—buy and bust, routine patrols, corner sweeps—have had little long-term impact in the Triangle and MLK, but have in some cases served as deterrents, police say. Other strategies, involving social service programs, job training, and intensive community involvement, brought better results.

Authorities and residents believe a unique, blended approach will be needed to address the conflict in the long term. That strategy, they say, will need to combine intensive drug-enforcement tactics that smother drug markets with social service programs that offer gang members alternatives to dealing. Such a program, they hope, can serve as a national example for other suburbs trying to end Bloods-Crips conflicts.

To find a model for that sort of multifaceted approach, they won't have to look far.

"We already did that sort of thing right here in Hempstead, in what was then the worst open-air drug market on Long Island," village police chief Michael McGowan says.

Hempstead mayor Wayne Hall (left) and police chief Michael McGowan discuss ways to end the 2012 gang war. "We want people to feel safe in their community," Hall says. "And we won't stop until they are. We owe that to them."
KEVIN COUGHLIN

In the summer of 2007, Hempstead police and Nassau prosecutors launched the Terrace-Bedell Initiative, a massive enforcement effort aimed at cleaning up the drug market at Terrace Avenue and Bedell Street. At the time, Terrace-Bedell, or "Terror Avenue," as locals called it, was the largest drug bazaar on Long Island, with more crack and weed moving through it than the Triangle and MLK markets combined. The initiative incorporated a blend of zero-tolerance drug policy with social service assistance.

Miraculously, where dozens of previous police crackdowns launched in the market's three decades of operation had failed, this one worked. Within a year of the operation's start, the neighborhood saw a whopping 87 percent reduction in drug crimes. Overall, crime in the Terrace-Bedell community fell by 73 percent in 2008.

"We knew that if we could dismantle the market, the violence would also decrease," Nassau County district attorney Kathleen Rice said after the operation.

The basis for the Terrace-Bedell Initiative was something called the High Point strategy, developed by criminologist David Kennedy. It advocates taking down a neighborhood's most violent dealers, while at the same time inviting nonviolent dealers to a "community intervention" where their families, friends, and neighborhood leaders tell them it's time to change their ways—or go to prison. Support for the dealers is offered in the form of medical, educational, vocational, and other social services. Simultaneously, heavy police resources are called in to close down the drug market, essentially occupying the neighborhood until all traces of dealing—each and every corner boy and crack house—are gone.

After consulting with Kennedy, police and prosecutors began collecting evidence against major dealers on Terrace-Bedell, identifying about fifty of them. More than thirty-five of those dealers, deemed the worst of the bunch by authorities, were prosecuted on drug charges. Thirteen others with mostly nonviolent histories were "given a one-time offer to go straight," or be prosecuted for dealing drugs, prosecutors said. All thirteen took it, receiving job training, addiction treatment, educational assistance, and behavior modification counseling. These services were also made available to the community at large, giving residents further incentive to work with law enforcement.

"It was a tremendous success and solution to what had been a terrible problem in that neighborhood," Hempstead mayor Wayne Hall says.

With all major dealers removed from the drug market, police increased their presence, arresting replacement dealers and drug users for even minor infractions. Simultaneously, prosecutors and the Long Island Building and Trades Union launched an apprenticeship training program for dealers interested in careers in construction and trades. Many found jobs and gave up slinging for good.

"Our goal was for the police to provide such a presence that the community would eventually be able to stand up to the dealers, the loiterers, the vandals, and say 'We don't want you here,'" Rice said.

By the time the Terrace-Bedell Initiative wrapped up, the drug market was a shell of its former self. Dealers who still worked there did so out of sight of police, and residents who suspected dealing in certain buildings routinely notified cops—a trend that would have been unheard of in 2007.

But the operation was not without negative consequences. Upstart gangs, independent dealers, and Bloods and Crips corner crews who would likely have conducted business along Terrace-Bedell turned instead to the Triangle and MLK. As a result, the neighborhood succeeded Terrace-Bedell as Long Island's largest open-air drug bazaar. Today, it remains the area's longest continuously operating cocaine market—at three decades and counting.

"That market has existed there [the Triangle] for a long time, but it's grown," Mayor Hall says. "We have to figure out how to shut it down the way we did Terrace-Bedell. And a blended approach is probably the ultimate answer. We want people to feel safe in their community. And we won't stop until they are. We owe that to them."

Technology, too, will play a role in that blended approach, authorities say. Nassau Police are one of the first agencies in the country to place predictive analysis—the digital dissection of police data to predict likely offenses, their locations, and even perpetrators—at the center of their overall crime-fighting strategy. They expect it to become a key weapon in their efforts to stop Bloods-Crips conflicts, and perhaps to serve as a model for other predictive policing programs around the country.

"We're going to use everything at our disposal," Hall says. "Including technology."

The idea of forecasting crime in order to stop it before it happens may sound like science fiction, but it's a real system anchored in mathematical analysis, and it's transforming the way police fight crime on

Long Island. Nassau police officials grew so confident in their predictive analysis program that they recently replaced the department's longtime, run-of-the-mill crime-mapping and statistics program, called Nass-Stat, with Strat-Com, which makes predictions about future crimes based on reams of intelligence and historical data. In a few years, police believe, the system will be capable of alerting cops to which gangbanger might be planning a shooting, and who their target might be. It will even take into account potential motives.

"This is starting to change the way we do our jobs and the way we approach gang violence," says Detective Sergeant Patrick Ryder, head of the Nassau County Police Department's intelligence section. "These are tools we've never had before. Now that they're here, we can actually predict what's going to happen and stop it before it does. We have a chance to get to the spot before the gangbanger does."

Nassau police have also begun hiring former Department of Defense analysts to staff their intelligence bureau, bringing the same level of network analysis performed by spy agencies to the county's antigang effort. In doing so, they've stopped treating the gang conflict like an isolated crime issue and started seeing it for what it is: a war. Working with Hempstead police, the unit's members use tens of thousands of arrest records, field notes, intelligence reports, and other source materials to create detailed maps of gang networks. These analyses identify gangsters' relationships to one another, the roles in their respective organizations, favorite dealing spots, and other illuminating details about their criminal networks. In this way, the gangs are being scrutinized as closely as terrorist groups, and with similar technological tools.

Police computers beam that data to monitors in each of the department's squad cars, giving beat cops detailed dossiers on gang members, along with their mug shots, in real time. The predictive analysis program also supplies units with up-to-the-minute information on hot spots—streets, corners, and even specific addresses—where gang shootings are likely to occur. From there, the program identifies "hot people" likely to commit gang-related crimes.

"We're able to determine not only the hot locations, but also some of the bad actors, before they have the chance to act," Ryder says. "And that's going to affect the gangs in a big way. When it comes to these conflicts, this technology is definitely a part of the solution. This is one of the tools that's going to help us beat these crews. But we're still figuring out the most effective ways to use it."

In the meantime, law enforcement agencies around the country watch to see what works in Hempstead, and what doesn't. Residents in every gang-plagued suburb-turned-war-zone keep praying things don't get any worse. And the Bloods and Crips, as they have since their arrival in LA in 1969, stand their ground.

"Whatever people try and do with us, we ain't going to get shook," says Tyrek. "Either way, we ain't going to quit slinging. Because this shit right here? This Crips and Bloods shit? This is forever."

CHAPTER TWENTY

Aftermath

You put me in a quiet place, no beefs, no slinging, man, I'd go crazy. But all this *craziness? This I know.*

—J-Roc

"Like a ghost town," Tony says on a freezing night in February 2014, while surveying Mike Clary's old block. "Except for the homies."

He's on his way home after a day of meetings with Crips suppliers and strategy sessions with Tyrek. After months of diminishing profits due to the conflict with the Very Crispy Gangsters and the Bloods, things are nearly back to normal for the crew. Several VCG leaders and Bloods soldiers had been arrested as part of an antigang operation by the NYPD and Long Island authorities, effectively ending their all-out, double-team campaign against the Crips.

The Crips, too, had been dealt a blow by law enforcement, seeing more than a dozen members from across Long Island—including Rock, Dice Beckles, and Skinny Pete—arrested in April 2013 in what the FBI and Nassau County authorities hailed as the county's largest-ever gang takedown. The charges ranged from attempted murder and robbery to drug dealing and selling guns. Several gangsters were also arrested on homicide charges for killings that took place in 2012, and are awaiting trial.

"We got a lot of hustlers," says Delahunt. "But it didn't really change anything."

Younger Crips have been promoted to replace their arrested colleagues. And with their enemies weakened, money is again coming in faster than Tyrek and his men can spend it. After months of uncertainty, the gang's expansion to New York City appears a success—despite the toll it's taken.

"It was worth it," Tyrek says. "Sometimes you've got to battle your way into new markets. And you've always got to deal with police. Ain't nothing free, ain't nothing easy. This is a business, and war is a part of our business that has to be dealt with if we want to stay on top. To be honest, a war economy is good for us, because it makes the drug dealing the lesser of the evils. When people getting shot, nobody cares about the drugs getting sold behind those bodies. They just care about the bodies."

And so the Triangle war, nearly three years after it started, drags on. In place of the old model of all-out battle between the Crips and Bloods, a new status quo has been established—one of permanent, low-intensity conflict. The gangs, pipeheads, police, and law-abiding citizens all seem to accept this as the "new normal" in and around the Triangle, because "it's better than what came before, which was like a Little Fallujah," Delahunt says.

Even Reverend Lyons, whose efforts recently led to the closing of the Bloods' old meeting spot, Seduccion, concedes only so much can be done. "When we're there [in the Triangle], we make an impact," he says. "But we cannot march twenty-four hours a day."

J-Roc's small but plucky Bloods set is still slinging on a few MLK corners. And shootings, stabbings, and homicides involving the rival sets are still regular occurrences. They've hated each other for so long, J-Roc says, it's only natural they "clap at each other" now and again.

"It ain't never going to end, now I'm sure of it," says Donna Crawford, whose only surviving son has begun dealing drugs part-time with J-Roc's crew. "The Triangle, I believe, will always be dangerous and full of drugs and Bloods and Crips. And it will always swallow up our children. It's already taken two of my boys, and it's got its hooks in the third, because it's a cursed neighborhood . . . a little piece of hell right here in Long Island."

The Bloods-Crips conflict remains a constant threat to kids who must walk through the Triangle to get to school; to residents who must drive through drug markets to get to work; to gang members and noncombatants suffering from PTSD but unlikely to ever be treated; to women at constant risk of sexual assault because of where they live.

The hustlers still hustle. The pipeheads still cop. Bullets still fly. In one of the wealthiest counties in the country, this bleak routine plays itself out day after day, with no end in sight.

"We can't give up," Mayor Hall says.

But some already have.

Like Delahunt, who will start a job in 2015 with another police department, far from Hempstead. "You get to accept these horrible things, because they become so common," he says of violence in the Triangle. "People can learn to live with pretty much anything. That's what I learned, spending my career here."

Delahunt and Clary say they don't feel guilty about leaving the neighborhood, believing they did everything in their power to salvage it. Even with the efforts of Lyons, his marchers, and other "true believers," Delahunt says, the Crips and Bloods appear no closer to giving up their way of life. If anything, surviving the game as long as they have has strengthened the current crop of hustlers' commitment to the drug business.

"We accepted that the desire of the Bloods and Crips to keep up their beef and keep moving their product was greater than any efforts we could possibly make," Delahunt says. "I think that moment came for Clary when his car got shot up. For me, it was when Devon got shot. Of all the kids I thought would escape that life and go to college, become something more, he was the one I thought had the best chance. And they took that from him. So no, I don't feel like we're giving up; I feel like we ran out of answers. There's a difference."

For Hempstead's gangs, perpetual warfare is "all we know," says J-Roc, who still walks with a practiced limp in imitation of Ice. "If we wasn't shooting and grinding, what would we be doing? This is how it's been out here since I was a little kid. Ain't no other way to be. You put me in a quiet place, no beefs, no slinging, man, I'd go crazy. But all *this* craziness? This I know."

Even those who escape the Triangle are not always able to forget their old beefs nor their desire for revenge. Steed, working as a cook in a New Jersey fast-food joint, says he thinks every day about returning to the Triangle to avenge Patrice's stabbing and the baby he lost. He fantasizes about killing Tyrek so often, in fact, he believes the murder inevitable.

"As much as I wish I could forget it, I can't," he says, touching his scar. "I'm not a father because of him, because he took the life of my unborn child. And he took from me the woman I was down for, someone I really loved, who had my heart. I ain't met anyone like her. On top of that, that nigga's people did Big Mac, Doc, Lamar, Super Curt, *and* Ice. Almost got me, too. So I'll most likely come back on his ass one day. Can't see a way not to. I got my life together here, yeah. I got my GED with Willie's [William Ricks's] help, got a decent job, but I don't never forget. A man do you like that, he gots to get got. Maybe next week. Maybe next year."

But Steed never gets the chance. On a snowy night in early 2014, he's found dead of a gunshot wound on a desolate street corner in Camden, New Jersey. He'd been on his way to sign up for an SAT prep exam—the first step in what William Ricks had hoped would be Steed's pursuit of a college education.

Most of Steed's friends suspect that Rock, freshly released from jail, carried out the hit on Tyrek's orders. But the Crips refuse to say whether they orchestrated the killing.

"It don't matter who shot him," Tyrek says. "I'm just glad somebody finally put that sorry nigga out of his misery. Like I said, he should have stayed in LA."

When no family members come forward to claim Steed's body—his mother dead of cancer, his siblings estranged from him for years—William Ricks and Calvin Bishop drive out to Jersey to identify him.

"This young man laying here makes me feel like we failed," Bishop says after seeing Steed. "Lord help us."

That same night, a pair of shots rings out as Tony hurries down Linden Place, but he doesn't flinch. The near-daily gunfire in the Triangle is nothing more than background noise to him now. He's got more important things to worry about anyway, he says, having just received news his girlfriend's in labor at Nassau University Medical Center. He speeds to the hospital and gets to her room shortly after his second son, Anthony Sherman III, is born. She hands Tony the dozing, seven-and-a-half-pound newborn. He kisses him on his forehead.

"I'm your pops," Tony whispers. "You going to have a lotta heart, be a hard little nigga, I can tell."

The baby begins to cry and Tony hands him back to his mother. He says he has forgotten something in the car, hurries down to retrieve it. When he returns, he's holding a gift for his son—a onesie in sharp Crips blue that his godfather, Tyrek, purchased for him. He insists on changing the boy into it.

"He going to be just like his pops," Tony says, pulling the onesie over his bawling son's head. "My little soldier."

A Note on Sources

My research for this book began in January 2012 while working for the New York *Daily News*. I covered the paper's courts beat in the Bronx, where thousands of Crips and Bloods live and fight. Accordingly, I attended many legal proceedings involving the gangs' members. I also spent countless hours at crime scenes, plodding through bloodstained streets, learning about turf lines, and picking up gangland gossip wherever I went. In this way, I got a primer on the brutal worlds both gangs inhabit and developed a fascination with their long-running conflict.

At Bronx Supreme Court, where I spent my workdays, fights between Bloods and Crips regularly broke out in courtrooms and hallways. Things got so bad that some judges prohibited court attendees from wearing red or blue. Others had extra sets of metal detectors installed directly outside their courtrooms when Crips or Bloods were on trial. During one such proceeding, a city police detective I knew—and whom I frequently used as a source—was on hand to testify for the prosecution. He pulled me aside outside the courtroom one day and told me about a Bloods-Crips conflict even bloodier than the ones I'd been covering.

"It's real bad," he said.

"Where is it?" I asked. "The Bronx? Brooklyn?"

"Long Island," he said. "They're fighting over a piece of territory called the Triangle."

"Bodies?"

"Oh yeah. Bodies. Crack. Guns. All in the 'burbs."

The next day, I made the twenty-two-mile drive from the Bronx to the Village of Hempstead, following a map the detective had drawn for me. The well-manicured lawns and upscale shopping centers dotting most of Long Island's streets quickly gave way to run-down buildings and abandoned homes in Hempstead. Parts of the village remained relatively safe, their streets lined with pharmacies and sandwich shops. But a large swath of it embodied the very picture of urban blight, its streets dirty and decrepit, its decayed housing stock more reminiscent of the South Bronx than the rest of Long Island.

Even so, when I arrived in the Triangle, I thought I'd taken a wrong turn. The neighborhood had the look and feel of a drug market—narrow roads, long-abandoned houses, drug baggies and vials strewn about—yet it was empty, not a single corner boy in sight. There were two schools located almost directly next door, as well as a playground. Surely Long Island crack dealers wouldn't be so brazen as to sling in sight of kids walking to class or children at play.

I made a U-turn with the intention of circling back onto the main road. It was there, at the corner of Linden Avenue and Linden Place, that the Hempstead Crips appeared. Three of them strode out into the middle of the street, gesturing for me to roll down my window. They knocked on the hood of my car, as if in greeting.

"What you need?" one of the Crips said. "Yayo? Rock? Some weed? Come on, yo, ain't got all day."

I looked past the Crips who'd come out to serve me. Five or six of their brethren shifted about on a Linden Place stoop, watching me closely, seemingly ready to join their homies in the street if anything went awry. I told the touts I wasn't looking to cop.

"I'm a journalist writing a story about the Linden Triangle," I said. "Is it all right if I hang out with you guys for a little while?"

Before I could say another word, they were shouting curses at me. One accused me of being an undercover narcotics cop. Another leaned in through my open passenger window and said, "Nigga, you best leave right now."

I drove off to the sound of them jeering. In my rearview mirror, they saluted me with middle fingers, hawked loogies in my direction, and grabbed their crotches. All in all, I thought, my introduction could have gone a lot worse.

"Shit, you're lucky they didn't shoot your white ass," my detective source said when I told him about the encounter. "Maybe you need a different approach."

As winter wore on, other stories took precedence. Fresh murders needed covering in the Bronx each day. So did trials of the accused. I put the Triangle story on the back burner, promising I'd come back to it during a lull on my beat. Not long after, I got a call from the managing editor of *Newsday*, Long Island's Pulitzer Prize–winning daily newspaper, offering me a job covering criminal justice. I'd applied months earlier, fascinated by the island's salacious murders, drug epidemics, and gang problems. Hungry to explore the seedy underbelly of suburbia, I accepted the position and immediately delved back into the Triangle story.

I started by attending a Hempstead community meeting, organized by Triangle residents concerned about the recent gang violence. They complained of drug dealers swarming their cars and making aggressive sales pitches, just as the Crips corner boys had done to me weeks earlier. The residents said gunfire was so common in their neighborhood they didn't let their children outside after dark. Some even hid their kids in the bathtub when bullets started flying. And they always kept their windows closed, lest a stray slug find its way inside amid a Bloods-Crips gun battle.

"I've been trying to get through to these young men for a long time," Male Timmons, the leader of a local neighborhood association, told me after the meeting. He'd been shot at while trying to make peace between the gangs, but that hadn't deterred him. "We have something new going on now. We're doing prayer marches. Why don't you come out and see for yourself?"

He gave me the number of the man in charge of the marches, Reverend Kirk Lyons, a fifty-one-year-old Hempstead native who ran a ministry with locations in Newark, New Jersey, and Brooklyn, New York. Some of Lyons's old friends had called to alert him to the Bloods-Crips gang war ravaging his hometown. He'd agreed to come home to try and calm the violence. When I called him, he said I was welcome to march with his men, with one caveat: I ought to be ready for anything.

"We march at midnight," he said. "One side of the neighborhood is Crips. The other's Bloods. We're walking through both."

I joined the marchers that Friday and many others, rain or shine, walking through Long Island's largest, most dangerous open-air drug market. I observed their prayer circles, and sometimes participated in them, holding hands with the gang members, addicts, and prostitutes they prayed with. One night, I held the hand of a young Crips associate, just a child, his palm small and sweaty. He wore expensive Nike high-tops and a kid's-size basketball jersey. I wondered how he'd ended up working a drug corner.

"Keep praying for me," he told me as I walked off. I told him I would. A few weeks later, I heard he'd been wounded in a gang shooting in Brooklyn. A bullet fragment had penetrated his eye, blinding him. On another march, I'd met a pretty young woman trying to beat heroin and cocaine addictions. At her request, I'd given her the number of a treatment hotline. She thanked me with tears in her eyes, gave me a hug. Two weeks later, she died of an overdose.

Every week brought more heartbreak: murders of Bloods and Crips, wounded children left handicapped, addicts lost to the needle or pipe. But the marchers never relented. They came to walk and pray every week. Gradually, both gangs came to trust them. In time, they came to trust me, too.

"If you going to write about our lives," Anthony "Big Tony" Sherman, the Crips lieutenant, told me one day over breakfast at a Hempstead diner, "you need to tell it right."

He and Flex Butler, then the set's third-highest-ranking member, had agreed to meet there after determining with certainty I wasn't a cop. The first few times they'd seen me on marches, they looked at me with contempt, probably recalling my initial drive into their territory. Lyons and others in the neighborhood vouched for me, though, and after a few weeks, the gangsters accepted my presence. I'd join them in prayer circles just like the other marchers, and sometimes lag behind to ask a few questions. The gangsters bummed my cigarettes and called me "crazy whiteboy reporter." Since they seemed to defer to Tony on most matters, I did, too. He turned down my offer to buy him and Flex breakfast five times before he finally said, "Aight, but I'm getting lunch to go, too."

So we ate, and they told me their stories.

"Once you in the game, you in," Tony explained. "That's your family right there. You all are brothers, same as blood."

He said he made his first dollar acting as a lookout for the Crips, a job they tried him out for when he was twelve years old. He was told to whistle loudly three times and shout "Police!" at the dealers whenever cops headed their way. That was the signal to hide the stash, which, if seized, could land them all in jail and, more important to the gang's leaders, bring a heavy loss in profits.

"That's why lookout's so important, because that's like the center in football," Tony said between bites of his omelet. "Game can't be played without him doing his job, quarterback ain't get the ball without him. It's some basic shit. But essential, too. That's the first job the older niggas give you, to see if you can maintain. To see if they can trust you. Find out if you got a brain."

It was the first of many lessons I'd be given on gang protocols, history, rituals, and etiquette while interviewing Crips and Bloods, as well as the cops, activists, and addicts who peopled their world. I asked Tony if he'd be willing to let me spend weekends with his set to supplement the reporting I'd done during prayer marches. He agreed to take my request to Tyrek, leader of the Hempstead Crips.

"Nothing go down without his say-so," Flex said.

Just then, Tony's phone rang. It was one of those plastic disposables all the Bloods and Crips carried. They called them "burners" and usually burned through three or four a week.

Tony answered, listened for a few moments to whoever was on the other end, then said, "Do it."

He asked me to drop him and Flex off near the Triangle. Tony was making phone calls in my car the whole trip, giving instructions to various Crips. When we stopped at a light near the Triangle, the men got out. Tony gave me a final piece of advice.

"You'll want to stay far away from here tonight," he said.

Hours later, a Bloods associate was found dead of multiple gunshot wounds. The shooter or shooters were in the wind, police said. Whether or not Tony and his men were involved, I didn't know.

I got a call from him the following night.

"Tyrek say you good for this weekend," he said. "From there, we'll take it week by week. If you do some stupid shit, you out."

For the next year, I hung out with the Crips most weekends. They told me war stories, took me on missions, and gave me access to their world. It was more violent than I'd imagined, crueler than I thought possible.

The Bloods were a harder sell.

"Yeah, you can come around, but you get popped, it ain't on me," Michael "Ice" Williams, the Bloods leader, said after I'd spent two months pressing for interviews with him and his set. "If you make these niggas angry, I can't protect you. They don't like what you write? Shit, they might kill you just for that."

Despite those risks, I took the deal. On nights I wasn't hanging out with Crips, I immersed myself in the world of the Bloods. The access was unprecedented—an opportunity to cover an ongoing gang war from its front lines. But there were plenty of dicey moments, too. I found myself ducking as bullets flew around me on several occasions. I had guns pointed at me two other times—once during an attempted robbery on my way home from an evening with the Crips, and another time by a Crips member himself. He'd gotten so high he'd convinced himself I was an undercover FBI agent posing as a journalist. In his stupor, he also believed I was the Hempstead police chief's adopted son. These paranoid thoughts led him to stick a revolver in my face, an act for which he later apologized.

It was one of dozens of times various gangsters, addicts, and community members accused me of being an undercover. To negate their suspicions, I spent as much time around them as I could, showing folks pictures of my family, bringing them copies of newspaper stories I'd written, telling them jokes, talking sports. I said nothing that got anyone arrested. I never discussed any of their conversations or activities with police. In time, most people came to realize I was probably who I said I was: a journalist who wanted to write about their unique world. A "crazy white boy," yes, but not a cop.

My goal was to delve as deeply as possible into the local Bloods-Crips war and, in doing so, to understand what has fueled the broader, forty-five-year-old conflict. To do so, I focused on the day-to-day decision-making processes of both Hempstead sets, analyzing each tactical move and strategic shift. I approached my coverage as a reporter would any complicated conflict, focusing on both sides' strategies, goals, and motivations; daily battlefield developments and atrocities; impact on civilians; and the involvement of law enforcement officials.

I also sought to tell the story of the Bloods-Crips conflict in terms of its human costs. No gang war in this country has dragged on as long or caused so much trauma, both physical and mental. The death toll, more than twenty thousand lives lost in forty-five years, is astonishing. Yet the Bloods-Crips war, as a whole, receives scant coverage in the press. Residents in war-torn communities say that's because nearly all those killed or wounded in the conflict are poor and African American. But it's also due to the nature of the battle. It is dangerous to cover, difficult to track, and even harder to make sense of. For those reasons, I felt the only way to do the story justice was, as Reverend Lyons said, to "get in close" and track it in real time.

In exploring the plights of gunshot victims, rape victims, and sufferers of PTSD, I tried to deal with the subject matter as sensitively as possible, while also examining the issues in the broader context of the Bloods-Crips conflict. As for the victims of sexual violence who shared their stories in these pages, each is more courageous, in my mind, than anyone caught up in this senseless feud.

Just one article about the Triangle war had been published before. I wrote it in June 2012 for *Newsday*. The piece focused on village police redoubling their efforts to stop the Bloods-Crips battle, along with the actions of the prayer marchers. I'd planned to write more stories about the conflict, but as they had in the Bronx, breaking stories took precedence. I put my notes on the gangs aside, hoping to revisit the project one day.

Then, in May 2013, I got a call from Toni LaFleur. Her son Devon, a Bloods member on the verge of escaping gang life, had been shot by a Crips member and left partially paralyzed. I'd spent many hours interviewing him in the months before his injury. Toni asked me why I hadn't done anything more with the material I'd gathered—why I hadn't told the story of her son, and so many others whose lives had been destroyed by gang violence.

"If a journalist on Long Island isn't going to tell this story, who is?" she said. "If you don't care enough to write it, it means no one will ever care. It means no lessons will be learned from all this pain."

I took Toni's words to heart. When we ended our conversation, I started writing. After hundreds of follow-up interviews and nearly a year of additional reporting, this book was born.

As for methodology, I mostly conducted interviews on the fly, without any prearranging. I'd meet up with Crips or Bloods and follow them around with a notebook and pen. Same thing for the cops, activists, clergymen, crime victims, sexual assault victims, addicts, concerned citizens, and others I spoke with. In the midst of illegal activity, I usually put my reporting tools away, fearing they might inhibit the gang members or otherwise impact the natural course of events. I'd write down my recollections of those events later—not an ideal reporting method, but my best choice given the circumstances.

I saw 40 to 50 percent of the events chronicled in this book with my own eyes. The rest I reported through interviews with more than 250 people who'd been involved in the events, or otherwise witnessed them. Sometimes, a shooting or other important development in the gang war would take place while I was doing reporting elsewhere. In my descriptions of those events, I've relied primarily on the accounts of gang members. As for the dialogue recorded in these pages, I heard much of it myself. In other cases, I reconstructed conversations as accurately as I could based on interviews with those involved. Beyond that, I've used interior monologues or referenced a subject's thoughts only in cases where I questioned them in detail about their thinking at a particular moment.

Gang members have a tendency to embellish, and some viewed the presence of a reporter as an opportunity to elevate their reputations on the street. As a result, I corroborated the anecdotes shared by Bloods and Crips whenever possible through the use of legal records and witness interviews. Since much of what took place during the Triangle war escaped the notice of law enforcement and the public, such corroboration could not always be found. Therefore, I've taken care to include only anecdotes I believe accurate. Many others have been excluded.

Throughout the reporting process, I tried my best not to insert myself into the events I covered. In that same spirit, I've chosen not to include myself in this narrative about the Bloods, Crips, and their world. The story is not mine; it is theirs.

A final word of disclosure: I did on occasion, though not without cause, help my subjects. I'd regularly give spare change, a few dollars, or a word of support to those who seemed legitimately in need. I also sometimes gave rides to subjects, saving them the cost of bus or taxi fare and using the trips as opportunities to interview them. In cases where addicts or gang members looked to me for information about drug treatment or social services, I provided it.

As for the names of people in this book, most have been changed to protect their identities. In exchange for anonymity, they granted me access. Some gang members agreed to let me use one of their street aliases (each typically has several). Others chose variations on their street names and agreed to be identified by those. A few people I met during the course of my reporting could not later be located to discuss these matters, sometimes due to their imprisonment or death. In such cases, I've chosen aliases for them. And in instances where gang members implicated in criminal activity were killed, I've identified them by one of their aliases rather than their real names, out of respect for their families.

Other than Hempstead police chief Michael McGowan and Nassau Police detective sergeant Patrick Ryder, all but one of the law enforcement officials mentioned in this book is quoted anonymously, since they were not authorized to speak with me. The lone exception was Detective Mark Delahunt, who chose that alias himself. (Delahunt didn't have approval from his bosses to speak with me, either, but his deep involvement in the gang war necessitated his being identified pseudonymously in the narrative.)

In regards to numerical data pertaining to the local and national Bloods-Crips conflicts, most of it is drawn from my analysis of multiple source documents and hundreds of interviews. The documents include annual gun crime statistics compiled by the New York State Division of Criminal Justice Services; incident reports and court records from

528 shootings in New York, New Jersey, Pennsylvania, and Connecticut; shooting statistics from the NYPD, Nassau County Police, and Suffolk County Police; local, state, and federal government data on gunshot injuries in all fifty states; thousands of newspaper and magazine articles; and interviews with more than 250 Bloods, Crips, and gang investigators.

For guidance on writing about drug dealers and gangs as well as information on those subjects, I found a number of works invaluable. Among them: *The Corner*, by David Simon and Edward Burns; *Do or Die*, by Leon Bing; *Dark Alliance*, by Gary Webb; *Gangs in Garden City*, by Sarah Garland; *Don't Shoot: One Man, a Street Fellowship, and the End of Violence in Inner-City America*, by David M. Kennedy; and "Cocaine Incorporated," a story by Patrick Radden Keefe published in *The New York Times Magazine*.

I've stayed in touch with some of the people mentioned in these pages. Devon LaFleur, who believes he'll one day walk again, is a continuous source of inspiration to me. He now lives with his mother in Brooklyn, where I have dinner with them every few months. When Devon talks about his days as a Bloods member, he doesn't sound bitter about what happened to him, nor does he appear to hold any rancor for Bolo Jay, the still-imprisoned Crip who shot him.

If anything, he smiles more now than he used to.

"I smile because I'm still here," he says. "A lot of my boys aren't."

ACKNOWLEDGMENTS

Any journalist reporting on the lives of gang members and drug dealers must rely on others to help them successfully navigate that world. In pursuing this story, I was aided by dozens of Long Island residents who introduced me to my subjects, taught me about their neighborhoods, vouched for my integrity, and tried to protect me during dangerous moments. Naming those kindhearted people might bring them unwarranted attention and risk, so I will refrain from doing so. But each knows the important role they played in making this book possible, and I thank them for it.

I also wish to thank my mother, Rita Deutsch; my grandmother, Bernice Shulman; my aunt, Lori Shulman; and my girlfriend, Laura Russo. Your support and enthusiasm kept me going during the hardest of times.

Thank you to my agent, Jill Marsal, and editor, Jon Sternfeld. Your wisdom and advice were invaluable.

Thank you to the Reverend Kirk Lyons, for inviting me on that first prayer march.

Thank you to Patricia Andrews, editor extraordinaire at the *Miami Herald*, for believing in me.

Thank you to my friends and colleagues at *Newsday*, who inspired me to give voice to the voiceless.

Thank you to my father, Howard Shulman, whose spirit is with me always.

ABOUT THE AUTHOR

Kevin Deutsch is an award-winning criminal justice writer for *Newsday*, and previously worked on staff at the New York *Daily News*, the *Miami Herald*, the *Palm Beach Post*, and the *Riverdale Press*. He specializes in journalism about street gangs, terrorism, and drug trafficking, and has received multiple prizes for his writing about crime and national news events. He lives in New York City.